Citizen
Governance

" . . . *whenever the people are well-informed, they can be trusted with their own government.* . . ."

Thomas Jefferson, 1789

Richard C. Box

Citizen Governance

Leading American

Communities

into the

21st Century

SAGE Publications
International Educational and Professional Publisher
Thousand Oaks   London   New Delhi

For information:

SAGE Publications, Inc.
2455 Teller Road
Thousand Oaks, California 91320
E-mail: order@sagepub.com

SAGE Publications Ltd.
6 Bonhill Street
London EC2A 4PU
United Kingdom

SAGE Publications India Pvt. Ltd.
M-32 Market
Greater Kailash I
New Delhi 110 048 India

Printed in the United States of America

Library of Congress Cataloging-in-Publication Data

Box, Richard C.
    Citizen governance: American communities in the
  21st century / by Richard C. Box.   1001684309
      p. cm.
    Includes bibliographical references and index.
    ISBN 0-7619-1257-6 (cloth: alk. paper).—ISBN 0-7619-1258-4
  (pbk.: alk. paper)
      1. Local government—United States—Citizen participation.
  2. Political participation—United States. I. Title.
    JS331.B68 1998
    352.14′0973—dc21   97-33722

98 99 00 01 02 03 04 10 9 8 7 6 5 4 3 2 1

Acquiring Editor:	Catherine Rossbach
Editorial Assistant:	Kathleen Derby
Production Editor:	Michele Lingre
Production Assistant:	Lynn Miyata
Typesetter/Designer:	Marion Warren
Indexer:	Julie Grayson
Cover Designer:	Candice Harman
Print Buyer:	Anna Chin

Contents

Foreword

In the early 1970s, I lived in a subdivision in a rapidly growing suburb of Pittsburgh. There was one street into the subdivision; every day, when the school bus stopped to let the kids off, the street was completely blocked. The community had a council-manager form of government, and many of the council members were representative of the "old" residents.

As the community grew, the need for an additional fire station became apparent. Acting on the advice of the Community Planner, the Council approved locating a substation just within the entrance to the subdivision on a piece of land owned by the deputy fire chief, one of the old residents (it was an all-volunteer force at the time). Two hundred residents of the neighborhood presented a petition to the Council explaining the problem with the school bus and asking why the station could not be located in a vacant field across the road form the subdivision. We were assured by the planner that zoning variances would handle any problems although he had never been on the street when the school bus stopped.

At the end of the meeting, the Mayor, a milkman by trade, thanked us for our participation and informed us that he was persuaded by the Planner because "he is our expert." Shortly thereafter I decided to go to graduate school so I could be an expert too. The Planner ultimately became vice president of the largest development corporation in the area. The fire substation was not built in the neighborhood.

This case illustrates many of the issues that Richard Box raises in this book—the citizen as outsider, the practitioner as expert, and the legislative body as representative of elite interests. The Community Governance Model outlined in this book would change those roles, making the citizens decision makers with the practitioner as expert adviser and legislators responding to the needs of all community residents.

Professor Box has drawn on his rich experience as a local government manager, coupled with his studies of democratic processes and public administration, to develop a model of governance which serves the public and, in its ideal form, enhances the professional life of practitioners. He readily admits that his is a normative vision of how local governments can be managed, but he sees it emerging all over the country as citizens insist on meaningful participation in the development and implementation of policies that affect their lives.

The Community Governance Model is carefully developed to address the traditional values of public administration—e.g., efficiency and effectiveness—while also involving citizens more dynamically in the process of governance. The primary role of the administrator is to ensure that the policy process is open and inclusive and to provide advice and technical assistance to citizens who have traditionally been left out of local government decision making.

The model is compelling to those of us who believe deeply in the basic concept of government by the people—democracy with all its flaws. Early in this century, public administration was developed to improve government by importing management principles from business. One of the most important principles was executive control over implementation decisions in order to maximize efficiency and minimize political interference. Ironically, the Progressives who espoused "good government" also created a governance model which excluded ordinary citizens and skewed democracy toward the interests of elites.

Richard Box is attempting to bring public administration back to democracy by drawing new roles for practitioners and citizens in the governance of their own communities. Pointing to the widespread distrust of government today, Box argues that the exclusion of citizens has diminished the expertise of practitioners and the legitimacy of legislators. The only way out of this dilemma is to restore democratic principles by giving citizens a positive, inclusive role in the policy process. Involving citizens in governance will develop greater understanding of the role of government in society, the complexities of policy development, the difficulties of achieving consensus among diverse interests, and the nature of the public administrator's job.

Box's vision is no panacea, however, and he identifies some of the risks involved in implementing the Community Governance Model. Citizens will be involved not only in developing policy but also in implementing it. This may be expecting a lot of many citizens who are less involved in civic affairs today than earlier generations. There is a greater risk for practitioners who may offend powerful elite interests by working with other citizen groups; and they will no longer have the politics-administration dichotomy to hide behind with its imprimatur of expertise. Community governance implies that no individual has the solution to community problems so that involvement with citizens is a necessary function of the practitioner's work.

I also worry, and continually remind Richard, about the narrow interests of communities. How can we in the broader community ensure that community governance does not devolve to the protection of parochial and exclusionary community interests? Isn't it easier to implement this model in the walled-in, economically elite subdivisions that are springing up all over the country? How will community governance serve the interests of the poor, the disabled, the "others" of our localities? How will communities expand their policy base to include the interests of the greater community outside their neighborhoods? How can community governance be implemented in the large urban areas of our nation?

This book presents a vision of how our country could work if citizens were invited into the process of governing. The answers to the questions above will come in the refinement of the model during implementation. The book should be read by public administrators, citizens, and political leaders who are truly committed to improving government. The principles outlined here should become a part of what we teach to our public administration students as we prepare them for the twenty-first century.

Democracy is a messy system at best and not designed to be efficient. Yet it is still the best form of government devised to date. The development of public administration diminished democracy by installing experts in government positions at all levels and disenfranchising citizens from much participation beyond voting. Even with all our management techniques to increase efficiency and efforts to reinvent and improve government performance, public trust in public administration is at a historic low. The Community Governance Model seeks to restore our faith in government by bringing citizens to the table and public administrators to a central role in democracy. It is worthy of our consideration.

—*Mary M. Timney*

Acknowledgments

Many colleagues, authors, students, citizen volunteers in communities, and historical figures have inspired this work. There are three individuals, one group of people, and some publishers I would like to thank specially for making the writing of this book possible.

Professor Henry (Budd) Kass read the manuscript several times over 2 or 3 years, making detailed and insightful comments that I took very seriously. At one point, when I thought I might abandon the project, his encouragement led me to try once more.

Professor Mary Timney has been kind enough to write the Foreword for the book. I asked Mary to do this for me because her view of American democracy is penetrating and critical in the best sense, with a strong emphasis on citizen self-governance and honest discussion of power relationships. When I write something normative I think what her reaction might be; though we might disagree, this internal dialogue serves as a compass for my work.

This is my first book. I came to scholarly work late in life, having been a local government practitioner for a number of years before I chose to become a teacher and writer. Publication of this book carries a special meaning for me because the intended audience includes people I care about very much: scholars, public service practitioners, students, and citizens who want to advance the cause of democratic community governance. I want to thank Catherine Rossbach, Acquisitions Editor, and Sage Publications, for making it possible not just to get the book into print, but to publish it with a company that has done much to advance the study of public administration.

The group of people I want to acknowledge are my students at the Graduate School of Public Affairs at the University of Colorado at Colorado Springs. Quite literally, the book could not have been written without them. This is because my thinking about the topics covered has been shaped by our in-class conversations and written dialogues, shaped both substantively and in terms of my conception of what students of public service need to know about the relationship between Americans and their governments.

Finally, I have used portions of my published papers in this book, in places excerpting the material directly as a springboard for new writing, in places revisiting and reworking the concepts from this earlier work. I wish to thank the following publishers for kindly giving me permission to use this material here (citations are in the reference list): Sage Publications for two papers that appeared in *American Review of Public Administration*; Professor Jong Jun and California State University, Hayward, for two papers that appeared in *Administrative Theory and Praxis*, the journal of the Public Administration Theory Network; and Marcel Dekker, for a paper that appeared in the *International Journal of Public Administration*.

One

Introduction: A Return to Original Values

The challenges facing those who participate in the governance of American communities seem overwhelming—cutbacks in national aid to local government, racial tension, insufficient resources for basic services, debates about the council–manager and strong-mayor systems, and many more. However, it is more the norm than the exception for local government to face challenge and turmoil in the history of community governance. The current challenges are vexing, but they also present exciting opportunities to improve public service.

This book has been written for people engaged in shaping the future of American public life in local areas, in communities in the broadest sense of the term. The focus is on cities, but the ideas are also applicable to neighborhoods, counties, and special purpose and regional districts, as well as to nonprofit organizations that interact with the public sector. The people involved include citizens, elected representatives, public service practitioners, and the academicians who study communities.

Nothing said here is startlingly new or original; the practice of community governance in America is centuries old and the accumulated body of knowledge and experience is substantial. (Notice that I have used the word *governance* rather than *government* or *administration*. This is intended to include the entire range of activities of citizens, elected representatives, and public professionals as they create and implement public policy in communities.) Many ideas being tried today in community governance have been tried before, to be discarded for innovations that were themselves discarded, only to appear later in different forms. So, though some of the ideas presented in this book may seem a little surprising, they are mostly extensions or adaptations of practices grounded in the history of the institution of community governance.

In this narrative, I bring together the history of the development of local government and community political life, current trends, and cutting-edge thinking about the roles of citizens, elected representatives, and public professionals. The result is a model of local government structure and policy making that emphasizes a balance between efficient, rational service provision and open, democratic processes that allow citizens to govern their communities.

The reader will not, it is hoped, find the book to be abstract or confusing in a way that makes it hard to read, or worse, irrelevant to the daily tasks of governing communities. This does not mean that the book is free of concepts that help us to understand the phenomena of daily life. Indeed, without concepts, theories, and models of reality, daily life appears to be a random series of happenings, and we become powerless to change it for the better. Concepts, theories, and models are powerful tools for shaping our behavior and the situations that surround us to conform with a vision of how things ought to be. To this end, the book aims to link theory and practice, a mutually beneficial relationship in which daily experience informs and allows for modification of theory, and theory permits daily action that is more focused and effective.

I had in mind four broad themes as I wrote the book. First, the attention Americans give to public governance is increasingly devoted to the local level, the place where people feel they can make a real difference in the conditions that affect their lives. As people turn their attention toward their communities, they return to values that come from the history of community governance. Three such values are local control of public governance rather than state or national control, small and responsive government instead of large and cumbersome government, and the public service practitioner as adviser and helper to citizens rather than as a controller of public organizations. A part of this shift in attention from national or state governmental systems to local governance includes skepticism about the idea, drawn from the private marketplace, that local residents are only *consumers* of public services, people who should be treated like *customers*. Instead, some local residents are returning to their earlier role as *citizens*, people who are the owners of the community and take responsibility for its governance.

(I will often use the term *public service practitioner* instead of *professional*. In general, the intent is to use *practitioner* when discussing full-time, career people who do public service work in communities. *Professional* is used when I wish to emphasize the difference in training and experience between practitioners and others who lack their in-depth knowledge of a specific area of practice.)

Second, we can use knowledge drawn from the history of community governance to improve today's communities. There is a history of people striving to determine the future of their communities, sometimes in the face of difficult economic and political circumstances. In the early years of the nation, local governments were created for many reasons, including religious solidarity, commerce, or security. They were often governed, as were the English localities from which colonists drew much of their knowledge of local government, by wealthy and prominent citizens. The nineteenth century brought wider citizen participation in local affairs and exciting innovation as people dealt with problems of industrialization and urbanization. These problems called for changes in the form and function of government, resulting in experimentation with the strong mayor, commission, and council–manager forms of government in the late nineteenth and early twentieth centuries. Today's challenges and debates over issues of governance grow from this history, and it offers us a guide as we move into the twenty-first century.

Third, an understanding of the political and economic nature of communities is valuable for those who take part in governance. The work of citizens who come together to shape community policy takes place in an environment different from that of states or the national government. Local places are influenced by economic, governmental, and social conditions beyond their control and they have limited resources to deal with many issues. Community political interaction is often face to face, and, despite the limitations of local governance, many local residents can take part in community affairs in a way that gives them the satisfaction of seeing concrete results from their efforts. In some places, community power structures are closed and uninviting to citizen participation, a legacy of the history of local control by the wealthy elite; to open new opportunities for citizen self-determination is one of the most exciting and important tasks of our time.

Fourth, successfully meeting the challenges of the future and doing the best job we can with our opportunities depends on being willing to adapt our roles to new circumstances. In the past two or three decades, trends have been developing in the roles of citizens, elected representatives, and public service practitioners that will likely shape the character of community governance in the twenty-first century. These trends represent a search for a different balance between rational, professional administration and democratic openness and public accountability. In this search, the developing shifts in roles are (1) citizens become governors of the community instead of its customers; (2) representatives coordinate the efforts of citizens instead of making their decisions for them; and (3) practitioners focus on helping citizens achieve their goals rather than on the control of public agencies.

Later in the book, I outline an approach to community governance that uses the ideas of returning to local values and the importance of knowledge of the history and the nature of communities to construct a model of the governance roles of citizens, elected representatives, and public service practitioners in the next century. Part description of changes underway, part prescription to guide our actions toward a meaningful goal, I hope the reader finds that the model, which I call *Citizen Governance*, provokes thought and inspires a sense of the importance of public service in American communities.

This chapter and Chapter 6 are designed so the reader can quickly grasp the basics of Citizen Governance. For greater depth of understanding, the reader may turn to Chapters 2 through 5. Let us now look more closely at the idea that greater interest in local, as compared to state or national, governance leads us back to values embedded in the history of communities.

The Three Returns to Values of the Past

Value of the Past Number 1: Local Control

In the 1980s, the Reagan administration advocated return of some national-level programs to state and local governments. This was not new; earlier administrations had made the same suggestion. As with those earlier administrations, Ronald Reagan did not succeed in making sweeping changes in the distribution of programs and services; it is difficult to alter a system of this size, given entrenched interests and concern about the effects of severing financial ties with the national government. Despite the apparent failure of national administrations to reverse the trend toward centralization of public services, during the 1980s the nation experienced the fiscal limitations we now take for granted, because there simply was not enough money to do everything we wanted to do. Along with the inefficiencies of large-scale social welfare programs and skepticism about government's ability to administer its programs successfully, the shortage of resources led Americans to expect less from the national government and to turn toward state and local government as the focus of their problem-solving efforts.

The phenomena in evidence of this turn back to local action include greater citizen activism and participation in local affairs; resurgence of *communitarian* sensitivity to the responsibility of local residents for taking care of their own problems; resistance to control of the local policy process by national or state officials or local economic and political elites; citizen-generated ballot measures on tax limitation, growth, and other issues; and open public participation and decision making about the future of communities instead of leaving such decisions to a few local leaders. Greater citizen attention to community affairs demonstrates a return to a vision of citizenship characteristic of the era when Americans were creating the nation, the late 1700s. Thomas Jefferson believed in a vision of governance for America centered on small local governments, with states and the nation performing a limited number of very specific functions that were essential (like national defense) and hard to perform at the local or state levels. Jefferson's preference reflected a fundamental American value—reliance on self and community—or, put another way, local control as contrasted with identification with large and distant places and units of government.

The basic American value of local control was displaced by large-scale governmental action in the twentieth century, action that accompanied rapid urbanization and industrialization of American society. Local government, which had been the center of governmental revenue raising and expenditure as the twentieth century began, became by the later part of the century a much smaller part of total governmental expenditures and was heavily dependent for revenue on funds raised by the national government, then distributed to states and localities in the form of intergovernmental assistance (Nice 1987, 45–9). Because of the increasing scarcity of resources, local governments came to compete fiercely with each other for the jobs and economic stimulus created by the expansion, relocation, and building of new facilities by private firms and government agencies. This led to *anticipatory anxiety* (Logan and Molotch 1987, 294), in which communities attempted to outbid each other by luring firms with tax breaks, land, infrastructure, training programs in public colleges, and so on, even when firms would choose a particular community without such incentives.

In the midst of this shift from local independence to dependence, there were people such as American philosopher and educator John Dewey who recognized that "the family and neighborhood, with all their deficiencies, have always been the chief agencies of nurture, the means by which dispositions are stably formed and ideas acquired which laid hold on the roots of character" (Dewey 1927/1985, 211). Dewey thought that "democracy must begin at home, and its home is the neighborly community" (218). He was an optimist, refusing to believe that modern urban–industrial society prevented recapturing earlier values that tended to be ignored in such a large-scale, mass society.

He wrote of the "void left by the disintegration of the family, church and neighborhood" that "there is nothing intrinsic in the forces which have effected uniform standardization, mobility and remote invisible relationships that is fatally obstructive to the return movement of their consequences into the local homes of mankind" (215). He foresaw a future in which the standardized aspects of industrial–consumer culture could free people from worry about the basics of survival, allowing them to realize their full potential as individuals. Modern mobility, rather than being destructive of community feeling, may contribute new ideas, "preventing the stagnancy which has attended stability in the past" (216).

In the emerging twenty-first century environment of return to the value of local control, people in communities choose the extent to which they depend on state and national agencies and the amount of time, energy, and resources they are willing to devote to economic competition with other communities. Not everyone believes that physical or economic growth is the best thing for their community, and not everyone who thinks it is believes that government should be the vehicle for promoting such growth. Where people come together to collectively decide on the future of their communities in the twenty-first century, they will be more likely to question the old certainties of economic development and physical expansion, to give weight as well to concerns about air and water quality, school capacities, social inequality, infrastructure costs and traffic congestion, and the aesthetic character of their living environment.

In many places, this renewed sense of local control has taken hold in the past decade or two, and in some areas it has become a matter of statewide concern (Gale 1992; Nelson 1992). This public sense of greater control through knowledge and participation may be taken as a given in the next century. It could significantly change the relationship between elected officials and the general public and between public professionals and both their elected superiors and the public. The process of deciding the future of the community could look less like determining what business leaders want and whether any sizeable opposition exists, and more like a community dialogue in which "citizens and administrators . . . join to decide what to do and to act together for the public good" (Stivers 1990, 96).

Of course, many public matters cannot be dealt with effectively at the local level. National defense, interstate relationships, and issues of national concern such as civil rights are examples of the need for national action. There are parallel examples at the state and regional levels of government as well. Also, many services are more effective if provided in larger organizations—that is, there are economies of scale.

Value of the Past Number 2:
Small and Responsive Government

Small and responsive government means government shaped in response to citizen desires for lean and efficient government. This is government that only does those things citizens want done and does so in a user-friendly manner rather than as a ponderous bureaucracy. In the twentieth century, Americans have, naturally enough, come to expect many problems of society to be solved by government. I say "naturally enough" because the challenges of controlling the excesses of the capitalist system, conducting wars, dealing with economic depression, building the physical infrastructure to handle rapid population growth, and preserving the environment were met by governmental action at all levels in the twentieth century. However, in the late twentieth century it has become clear that there are limitations to governmental action, limitations of competence, resources, and public willingness to allow greater government intrusion into the lives of individuals.

The daily-use language of public management shows the evidence of this new public sense that government should be smaller, more clearly matched to public wishes, and less intrusive into private lives. Some of the terms providing this evidence are *privatization of public services, public–private partnerships, entrepreneurism in public management, total quality management, customer service orientation,* and *reinventing government.* Each of these concepts shares some of the values of the Age of Enlightenment in the eighteenth century, the time of the founding of the nation. These values include self-reliance, individual liberty, and government that does only those things the majority of the public wants to pay for and that the private market will not do. Not all of these management concepts or individualistic values are good or useful in all situations. They can have a negative impact on valid public objectives and may conflict with other, more collectivistic founding-era values that emphasize cooperative action, personal commitment to participate in public governance, a sense of community, and dedication to public service.

In a public-governance environment shaped by these contending values, many citizens have a different view of the role of government than Americans have had for the past several decades, and some of them wish to take part in determining the way their communities are governed. Among other things, this means that often citizens, rather than elected representatives or public service practitioners acting alone, choose which public services they want, in what quantities, and how they want them delivered. They choose whether action on particular issues should be taken by individuals or neighborhood groups without expenditure of public monies or by local government with public expenditure. So, citizens are involved in finding the answers to questions such as whether to have a full-service park and recreation system or just a few parks in crucial areas; whether fire protection is provided by full-time paid personnel, volunteers, or a mixture;

whether to have a publicly owned community hospital, publicly operated refuse collection service, publicly run fleet vehicle repair and maintenance, and so on. Or, instead, will these services be operated by the private sector alone or in a contractual or mutual relationship with the public sector?

Of course, not everyone wants to be involved in solving neighborhood problems or working on questions of the size and scope of activities in their government, and many who would like to do so simply do not have the time. Even so, the return to the value of small and responsive government means that the public is less likely to passively accept the decisions of political leaders and public professionals about what government should do and how it should do it. Instead, the reality for the future may be that many citizens will choose for themselves what services ought to be offered through the collective service-delivery mechanism of government.

People are increasingly aware that government services are not free and that to decide to provide a service is to decide that each taxpayer in the jurisdiction must pay for that service. Unlike voluntary contributions to churches, health clubs, charitable organizations, and so on, when the citizens' elected representatives tax them to provide a service, everyone pays whether or not they believe their government should offer the service. This places an especially heavy burden of responsibility on elected and appointed officials. In this time of resource scarcity, taxpayer revolts, and public reaction to the size of government, it also makes likely constantly rising levels of public scrutiny and demand for direct participation in the decision-making process.

Value of the Past Number 3:
The Professional as Adviser, Not Controller

The effort to reform government in the late nineteenth and early twentieth centuries was driven by a belief in the application of scientific principles to the management of public organizations. Managing in a scientific, businesslike manner required getting politics out of administration, using trained professionals instead of political appointees to administer services. By the mid-twentieth century, this professionalization of public management began to produce citizen resistance to rational–professional management and a call for greater accountability to the public. Academicians studying public administration in local government found that elected officials and community members preferred public professionals to function as expert advisers and managers of daily operations rather than as leaders in forming a vision for the community and proposing public policies. On the other hand, although some research has found professionals in agreement with this citizen preference (Fannin 1983), many professionals view themselves as a center of policy activity, as initiators of public action (Loveridge 1971; Nalbandian 1989).

Americans have always been wary of control of government by elites, whether they are elites of money and power or of professional training. The need for professional direction of the process of building a modern urban–industrial society was obvious, but the focus of concern began to shift in mid-century to the political challenge of answering claims from a variety of different interest groups. In this diverse and rapidly changing political environment, the enduring value of democratic control again became apparent, along with the beginnings of a return to an earlier view of the professional or expert as adviser and helper rather than as controller of community governance.

This trend is likely to intensify in the twenty-first century as citizens become more deeply involved in community affairs, demanding greater accountability from public professionals. Citizens will likely be more aware of the structural options available to them in shaping their community government. The reformers of the turn of the twentieth century favored structures maximizing central control and efficiency, but the twenty-first century may see a continuation of the revival of experimentation with citizen-centered governance structures. Structures such as the council–manager plan can place elected officials in the position of reviewing the actions of professionals rather than formulating policy. Narrow and restrictive citizen involvement processes can place people in the position of protesting actions of government instead of participating in decision making. Structures that have these effects may be modified, moving toward those that emphasize citizen involvement and informed decision making by elected representatives. Community residents may take an active part in creating these new structures as they ask for governmental accountability and direct involvement in the delivery of public services. For elected leaders and public service practitioners, this means a flexible attitude toward change, shedding of protective feelings about personal turf, and a willingness to engage in open dialogue on issues facing the community.

The Downslope of the Wave of Reform

Historian Arthur M. Schlesinger suggested that American political history has moved in cycles since the founding of the Republic, alternating between periods of *public purpose* and *private interest* (Schlesinger 1986). Schlesinger's father originated this idea in 1924, identifying eleven cyclic periods up to that time and finding that "In six of the periods the object was to increase democracy; in five, to contain it" (24). The length of particular cycles of political history and their causes are debatable, but it seems clear, given the swings in governmental activity we have seen during the Eisenhower, Kennedy/Johnson, and Reagan years, that there are periodic changes in public attitudes toward government.

Writing in 1969 in *Public Administration Review,* Herbert Kaufman argued that America occasionally experiences shifts of values and that "the administrative history of our governmental machinery can be construed as a succession of shifts of this kind, each brought about by a change in emphasis among three values: representativeness, politically neutral competence, and executive leadership" (3). Kaufman viewed our "earliest political institutions" as reactions to "executive dominance in the colonial era," followed by "extreme reliance" on "representative mechanisms" in the nineteenth century, resulting in a negative reaction to "legislative supremacy" and the spoils system in which many administrative positions were filled on a political basis. This led to the reform efforts of the late nineteenth and early twentieth centuries, with stronger separation of politics and administration, merit-based personnel systems, and administrative centralization for efficiency (Kaufman 1969, 3–4).

In 1969, Kaufman saw a reaction taking place against the excesses of reform, with a move toward decentralization and greater citizen participation marking a shift to the value of representativeness. He assumed that this "wave of reform" would be followed by another in reaction to regional partisanship, wide variation in local practices, and so on; the new wave would emphasize politically neutral competence, with "a new generation of idealists" who would "elevate the quality, the consistency, the impartiality, the morale, and the devotion to duty of bureaucrats" by insulating them from "political heat" (12).

During the era of the Republic's founding, the Federalists and Anti-Federalists expressed deep philosophical differences about the nature of the relationship between government and the governed. These debates carried forward into the early years of the national government, with Alexander Hamilton advocating the view that the national government should be energetic and vigorous in addressing the nation's problems and Thomas Jefferson advocating the view that the best government is local, limited, and governed by educated and involved citizens (Matthews 1986, 86–9).

The question of the nature of government and its relationship to citizens became a focus of attention in local government in the late nineteenth and early twentieth centuries as reformers sought to eliminate control of urban areas by political machines (see Adrian 1988 for an excellent short history). The reformer's goals were to maximize economy and efficiency, to make cities "run like a business" (Stillman 1974, 20–2), and to serve "the public interest" instead of particular private interests. The reformer's objectives were separation of politics from administration, hiring experienced professional managers to deal with technical problems, and application of the principles of scientific management to public organizations (Ross, Levine, and Stedman 1991, 138). Underlying the conflict between machine politics and the reform impulse was a tension between the fundamental values of political responsiveness and rational–professional administration.

Among the specific means adopted by reformers to achieve their goals in communities were at-large and nonpartisan elections instead of election by subareas called wards or districts. At-large and nonpartisan elections were intended to promote a broad view of the community-wide public interest instead of the parochial concerns of neighborhoods. Other means of reform included implementation of civil service systems and experimentation with organizational structures. At first, reformers tried the *mayor–council* (or *strong mayor*) system in which the chief administrative officer is elected, then the *commission plan* in which the job of administration is shared by several elected commissioners, and finally the *council–manager* plan, in which the chief administrative officer is a professional appointed by the elected council (Stillman 1974, 11–5). The intent of these structural variations was to provide effective leadership to solve the pressing problems of the day, often physical problems of building adequate streets, sewer and water systems and other infrastructure, along with associated problems of management and coordination.

This drive to reform local government was largely successful. Many of the problems with the physical structure of cities were solved and the more extreme abuses of power associated with boss or machine rule are mostly gone. The reformers' preferred system of local governance, the council–manager plan, "underwent its greatest growth during two periods: the post-World War I decades, when the number of manager cities quadrupled (from one hundred to four hundred cities), and the post-World War II decades, when again the number nearly quadrupled (from six hundred to twenty-two hundred cities)" (Stillman 1974, 20). In the mid-1980s, the council–manager form was found in about one half of the 4,365 cities with more than 2,500 in population responding to a survey conducted by the International City Management Association (Adrian 1988, 10). Even in county governments, often characterized by fragmented administrative structures and a large number of elected leaders, the use of professional administrators has become commonplace.

However, resistance to professionalization of local government has been growing; the success of local government reform as a social–political movement has generated a counterreaction as the problems that made new systems so attractive are solved and the negative features of the changes wrought by reform become apparent. Part of the resistance to professionalism has shown itself in changes from at-large elections to district elections and from the practice of councils choosing mayors from among their members to mayors being elected directly by the voters [about two thirds of American cities with the council–manager form of government now have directly elected mayors (Protasel 1988, 811)].

Much of the resistance to reform structures has focused on the city manager as a symbol of professional influence in local government. In the 1950s, as the nation built the suburbs and the modern infrastructure of highways, water treatment systems, schools, and other services needed to accommodate population growth and urbanization, voices of protest were heard in reaction to perceived professional usurpation of democratic community control. In 1958, writing in *Public Administration Review*, Dorothee Strauss Pealy expressed a belief that the council–manager plan exhibited too much efficiency as opposed to politics. Pealy advocated a return to partisan elections and stronger mayors, reflecting the views of a person who had just been elected as mayor of Grand Rapids, Michigan. The new mayor said,

> It is human nature to aggrandize power and authority, and the manager, if the commissioners are slovenly, negligent or indifferent in their attitudes, has a tendency to usurp powers that belong to the grass-roots commissioners, even to the extent of advising on policy which is strictly within the province of the elected officials. This should not be tolerated. (214)

Since Pealy's article there has been much work done in this area. It is clear that, whether or not elected representatives like it, local professionals are deeply involved in formulating policy (see Svara 1990, ch. 6). Often, elected representatives do not like it. In case study research of a mayoral election campaign in the late 1980s, I found this newspaper quotation from a council member in a town of 50,000: "I don't want a city manager who is going to run the city. We (the council) need to take the initiative. I don't want the city manager to make the proposals about where we're going to go" (Box 1990, 158).

In 1988, Greg Protasel examined grass-roots citizen efforts to force changes in their communities by abandoning the council–manager plan and going to the mayor–council (strong mayor) form. He found that these movements happen most often in small cities where elected officials lack leadership skills and depend heavily on the manager, who then becomes a visible symbol of professional control of community government. An article by Rob Gurwitt in *Governing* magazine (1993a) discussed the increasing "lure of the strong mayor." The piece was sufficiently threatening to the International City/County Management Association, a managers' professional group, that they argued against Gurwitt with an article in their monthly publication, *Public Management*. The title was "Beware the Lure of the Strong Mayor" (Blodgett 1994).

Community discussion about change in the form of government is common in many places. Academic research into the politics of council–manager plan abandonment sometimes makes it appear that these are isolated instances, extreme cases, but this is not true. Political tussles between those who champion what they see as dispassionate professional management and those who favor what they see as democratic control of the public agenda are not at all unusual. In many places this discussion is an ongoing feature of local politics, sometimes a quiet murmuring, sometimes rising to the level of noisy public debate; this phenomenon has long been recognized in American communities (Stene and Floro 1953).

However fascinating this may be, we should not focus too much on city managers as we look at trends in local governance structures. The same broad questions of the relationship between the people, their elected representatives, and public administrators may be found at all levels in the local public agency (for a comparative study of department heads in mayor–council and council–manager structures, see Abney and Lauth 1986). Many public administration academicians seem to prefer a model of local government professionalism featuring wide policy-making latitude for administrators, on the theory that intrusion of citizens into daily administration ("micromanagement") produces irrational or inefficient outcomes. However, the cultural and social foundation of American local governance is not professional rationalism, it is democratic self-governance. The problem is that, "in changing the structure of government and professionalizing the bureaucracy, the reformers removed the government further from the people" (Ross, Levine, and Stedman 1991, 155).

People often become strongly emotionally attached to their communities, viewing them as a refuge from the larger urban setting, a place to concentrate on family life, and an opportunity to create the living environment of their dreams. If citizens believe that a professionalized governmental structure is taking away some of their democratic ability to control the character and future of a community, they may well take action to restore the lost control. There is no particular reason community residents should support a governmental structure that appears to deny them access to the policy-making process or that treats them as cases rather than as persons. Though professional administrators may view with dismay citizen efforts to make local governance more politically responsive, it has always been the purpose of local government to serve citizens of communities, not a professional vision of how public life should be run. People often believe they have valid reasons for resisting professional, rationalized administration. Whether or not this belief is sensible from a professional perspective, the citizens' community is, after all, their community.

Schlesinger's cycles of political history and Kaufman's value shifts are not necessarily reflected in all communities, though it is often possible to identify cycles, or waves, of reform effort at the local level. Martin Shefter (1985) examined recurring fiscal crises in New York that were caused by politicians who were trying to please various constituencies. Each time political favor-seeking drove the city to the point of financial crisis, business leaders would sweep the current politicians out of office and restore fiscal responsibility. H. Edward Flentje and Wendla Counihan (1984) documented waves of reform in Wichita, Kansas, as city councils hired "insiders" for the city manager's job when they wished to preserve the status quo, then brought in professional managers from outside when they wanted to initiate significant changes in policies.

Each community's political history, including waves of reform if there have been such waves, is unique. Nationwide, the balance between the value of professional, rational administration and the value of democratic openness and public accountability tilted strongly toward rational professionalism through much of the twentieth century, and it is now moving toward democracy. This decades-long "wave of reform" is much longer than Schlesinger's political cycles, which seem to alternate every 16 years or so, and it looks much like Kaufman's value shift. As the previous discussion indicates, we are now on the downslope of a long wave of local government reform, headed toward an uncertain destination. Kaufman suggested that value shifts are repeating cycles in which "innovators of tomorrow will defend many of the very institutions (as transformed in the course of current controversies) under attack today" (1969, 12). Schlesinger was careful not to characterize his cycles of history as repeating themselves like a pendulum moving back and forth between two unchanging political opposites; instead, he recognized that each cycle brings something new that changes the nature of society and politics. Though Schlesinger wrote about national politics, the same may be said of human history at any level—time brings the paradox of change that seems new even as it is repeating the patterns of the past.

This paradoxical mixture of old and new is probably an accurate description of the current movement away from professional rationalism and toward democratic openness. The movement of political and administrative events along the downslope of the wave of reform will almost certainly not take American local government back to a nineteenth-century sort of machine politics or blatant self-seeking use of government for financial gain. However, it does mean a turning away from the use of collective (governmental) solutions to every possible problem, toward a more complex response involving a mixture of public and private services and a variety of experimental management structures. This is a pattern of the relationship between Americans and government that predates the reform of the late nineteenth and early twentieth centuries, yet it has the flavor of the postindustrial period of the late twentieth and early twenty-first centuries. For people involved in community governance, it means redefinition of roles and processes of creating and implementing policy that are citizen centered rather than bureaucracy centered.

The Principles of Community Governance

The concepts of a return to values of the past and the downslope of the wave of reform have set the stage for our discussion of Citizen Governance. This is a model of the ways citizens, representatives, and practitioners can join together in governing communities so that the strengths of each are brought to bear in addressing the challenges of the next century.

I do not advocate a nostalgic return to an idealized vision of the past. Such an idealized vision can obscure the reality of limited access to public life by women, racial minorities, and the economically less well off that is characteristic of earlier periods. Nor does this book represent a desire to turn back the clock of technical or societal progress. That is not the point. The point is that we, individually and collectively, are free to make choices about where we wish to find ourselves on a continuum of self-determination and control of our local public life. As we enter the new millennium, there is evidence that many Americans are exhibiting a desire to move back toward the active end of this continuum after several decades of living at the passive end.

This book is an argument for a reasoned and realistic response to these trends by the field of public administration and by citizens who care about communities. The argument I present is descriptive—that is, it describes the past and present, using this knowledge to examine future trends and challenges in community governance. It is also normative, or prescriptive, seeking to discover how to meet these challenges and to shape the future as we choose. Suggested answers to the normative question of what should be done to meet the challenges are guided by four principles of community governance. The reader is asked to accept these principles as "given" for the purposes of the book, realizing that the choice of these particular principles, and the way in which they are used, reflect the author's judgment and personal preferences. Further, we should recognize that these principles are valid only for our time and place, for our nation and the time in which we live. They cannot accurately be assumed to apply to other cultures or eras. Though we may share some values with people from other times and places, often we do not, and to the extent we project our values onto others, we fail to understand them.

The principles discussed come from the development of American society over several centuries. They are not consensual principles agreed on by everyone, but have been since colonial times, and remain today, at the center of sometimes contentious debates over the "best" relationship between Americans and their systems of government. They come from the American experience of leaving the Old World for the New, settling the continent, and fighting several wars in the name of preserving a certain way of life. Contemporary Americans see the principles of governance differently than did people in the colonial era, the nineteenth century, or the early twentieth century, but there are continuities of understanding and meaning, shared ideals adapted to the circumstances of the times. I believe these four principles represent the historical, contemporary, and the evolving American spirit of local, democratic self-determination:

1. *The Scale Principle.* Many issues of public policy are best handled at the state or national levels of government. However, as a rule it is preferable to keep public decision making and policy implementation as close to the people who are affected by it as possible. This allows citizens to participate directly and meaningfully in self-governance. It also allows government programs to be flexible in response to change, retaining an immediate and rational relationship to the reasons they were created. Keeping

policy at the "smallest" level possible means assuming that neighborhood-level policy determination is best, if it fits the nature of the policy issue and alternative solutions, followed by the community-wide level if that is more appropriate, then regional action. If none of these will produce the desired result, then state or national options can be pursued. In short, when deciding about the level of government appropriate to solve a public policy problem, the scale principle calls for a bottom-up rather than a top-down process.

2. *The Democracy Principle.* The "best" public policy decisions are those resulting from public access to information and free and open discussion rather than the preferences of elite groups or deliberation limited to elected representatives. This principle places moral and ethical value on allowing people in their communities as much opportunity as they choose to exercise in shaping the future.

3. *The Accountability Principle.* Community residents are the "owners" of their communities, so they should be the people to make the necessary decisions about which public services to offer and how to operate them. Elected representatives and public service practitioners have important roles to play in community life, but they should be supportive of, rather than superior to, the roles of local residents acting together as a community. Achieving governmental accountability to the public requires that citizens be involved in the policy process along with representatives and practitioners, beginning with discussion of action options, to making programmatic decisions, to administering programs, and to making changes based on observed performance.

4. *The Rationality Principle.* In making decisions about public policies and programs, citizens, elected representatives, and public service practitioners should strive to understand and clearly express their values, assumptions, and reasons for the choices they make. Rationality in public policy making is not about thinking or acting in a precise, neatly ordered, unemotional, or predetermined way. It is about recognizing that public decision making is an important enterprise, one that deserves time, careful thought, opportunities for people to express themselves and to be listened to, and respect for the views of others.

The "Is" and the "Ought"

As mentioned previously, there are two sides to this book—the descriptive (what is reality, to the extent we can tell?) and the normative, or prescriptive (what sort of future ought we to have?). All research and writing has a purpose and a bias; the question is whether these are clearly identified. I have done my best to present descriptive material in a balanced way, distinguishing it from that which is prescriptive. Let me state my purpose in writing this book and my normative bias, as clearly as possible, so the reader is able to sense where the narrative attempts to describe reality (and how the description may be affected by the author's bias) and where it is largely prescriptive. I function within, and largely accept, the society in which we live, but like many people, I wish for improvement. The improvement I desire that relates to the subject of this book is greater citizen control of the process of making and implementing public policy in communities.

We cannot meaningfully examine the making of public policy without taking into account the nature of the social, economic, political, and administrative practices and institutions that surround us, that both allow us to act and constrain the ways in which we take action. These practices and institutions are the product of many years of decisions and actions taken by people sincerely working for what they believed to be the betterment of their communities. They allow for predictability and consistency in our lives, but they also draw around each of us boundaries of law, tradition, organizational structure, and public expectations of what is "right" behavior.

The United States grew from its origin as a place where people could escape the power and the enforced conformity of the European nation-states and churches. But those fleeing Europe brought with them ideas about organizing public life that shaped the ways they organized to govern themselves. And, escaping the power of nations and churches did not mean that the emigrants abandoned natural human tendencies to create hierarchies of authority and wealth in their new society. Like people in other places or at other times, they created systems of public governance that reflected the distribution of wealth and influence in society.

The story of the development of the American community is a story of enduring uncertainty and disagreement about the relationship between citizens and those who are chosen to govern. Who shall exercise legitimate authority and for what purposes? What is the role of the ordinary citizen in shaping the formal structures of governing institutions, in deciding what actions shall be taken, and in determining who benefits from, and who pays for, public actions? To what groups or individuals are public professionals accountable, and for what purposes do they serve them? Local communities tend to be dominated economically and politically by people who profit from transactions related to economic development and the use of land, through development, redevelopment, sale and rental, and providing support to those involved in such transactions (support people include lawyers, bankers, accountants, appraisers, real estate brokers, and others).

Many people who are not directly part of this local system of economic growth are affected by it on a daily basis. For example, the trade of retail business owners may vary with the economic vitality of the community, and elementary and secondary schools and colleges may experience changes in enrollment with fluctuations in economic conditions. Thus, business owners and people involved in education have a stake in the economic growth of the community, and this can be said of people in many occupations. Identifying an "elite" that controls the community for its own benefit is not always easy. Each of us must sort out and evaluate our own interests, deciding what we want for our community and what the tradeoffs may be between economic vitality and quality of life. The problem we grapple with is how citizens can do the work of democratic governance given the nature of our political and administrative systems.

This book is in part a description of models of citizenship, elected representation, and the practice of professional public administration, and in part an argument for changes in these roles and in the operation of local government. The description of historical development and the current situation is intended to be a fair presentation of the range of ideas in research and writing in these areas. No doubt the selection and description of materials is influenced by the author's personal orientation, or bias, which tends to be in the direction of a Jeffersonian view of democracy—one that builds from the bottom up rather than top down, that is decentralized and local, and that allows people to participate in governance rather than depending on the rich, the powerful, or the expert to do their public work for them. This may be contrasted (see Stillman 1995, ch. 7) with a Hamiltonian view of democracy, which includes a large and energetic national government linked to a thriving commercial economy and governed by the educated and expert. Nevertheless, the narrative offers a useful discussion of what we know about citizenship, representation, and professional practice in community life, providing references to additional information for those who want to explore these topics further.

The prescriptive part of the book is an argument for change in the way public policy is made and implemented in local government. The focus is on the internal governance of local public organizations. Much good work is being done nationwide to facilitate citizen governance outside public organizations, through neighborhood councils, creation of task forces and committees, and so on. However, for citizen self-governance to be fully realized, it must also move inside public organizations so that local residents are directly involved in creating policy and shaping the way it is carried out in the daily work of administrative agencies.

Today, there are demands for public organizations to operate more like those in the private marketplace, to be efficient and customer friendly, to contract out or privatize as many services as possible, to "reinvent" the way they function. These demands are about managerial practice, the technical implementation of public policy, and they are crucial to the study of public organizations. In this book, we examine the relationship between citizens and these managerial issues, but we go beyond managerialism, considering the broader community, or civic, perspective on creation of the public policies that set the boundaries for administrative action.

The prescriptions for change offered are directed in part to the roles of the people involved in community governance. In the ideal realization of the Citizen Governance model, many citizens become directly involved in decisions about making and implementing policy (at the same time recognizing that many will choose to remain uninvolved), elected representatives coordinate this citizen work rather than serving as primary decision makers, and public professionals assist the work of citizens rather than focusing on the control of public agencies.

In part the prescriptions discussed in the book are structural. Changes in the roles of citizens, elected representatives, and public professionals may work best if they are accompanied by changes in formal organizational structures. People often express their values about government through structure, as did those who drafted the Constitution when they created a government of "separated" powers, splitting the authority to govern between the legislative, executive, and judicial branches to avoid concentration of power. At the local level, those who advocated the council–manager plan in the early twentieth century saw the unitary, business-firm structural model as a way to run government efficiently, like a private business. As we move toward greater citizen control of creation and implementation of public policy in the next century, it is likely that structures of community government will evolve as well, with distribution of decision-making responsibility among a larger group of people serving in a variety of roles.

There are many alternative models of the future of community governance in the literature of public administration and urban politics. In this work, I suggest one way that the internal operation of community government can move in concert with the changes under way in American values, and I present alternative models in the descriptive part of my writing. However, I offer no apology for arguing in favor of my particular vision of the future of community governance. The prescriptive model offered here, Citizen Governance, does not call for radical change, nor is it a naive call for a communitarian, collectivist future. It is a view of local governance grounded in the personal and shared experience of doing professional community work, in the history, practices, and contemporary realities of local government, and in basic American values about the relationship of citizens and government.

Design of the Book

The chapters to follow examine the political and economic context of American community governance and the roles of citizens, elected representatives, and public service practitioners as we enter the twenty-first century. Chapter 2 describes eras in the development of the institution of community governance, exciting times of change and challenge that give us a rich legacy to draw from today. It also describes the nature of community power and how it affects people who take part in community life. This overview of the development and nature of communities lays a foundation for the discussion of Citizen Governance.

Chapters 3, 4, and 5 focus in turn on citizens, elected representatives, and public service practitioners. They draw the reader into contemporary debates about the relationships between these groups and their local governments. Contrasting views are presented of the roles of these people and of prescriptions for future action. The prescriptions are designed to fit with the values of the past described previously, the nature of communities described in Chapter 2, and the scale, democracy, accountability, and rationality principles. In this way, the book addresses the questions, "What will be the challenges of community governance?" and "What should be done to meet these challenges?" with a three-pronged approach to citizenship, elected service, and professional practice called the Citizen Governance model.

Two

The Nature of
Community Governance

**Describing the Institution
of Local Governance**

A good place to begin an examination of the nature of community governance is to describe how it serves as an institution in our lives. An *institution* is a large and enduring set of practices that we accept, take for granted, because these practices are so familiar and so much a part of daily life. Philip Selznick wrote that, "a social form becomes institutionalized as, through growth and adaptation, it takes on a distinctive character or function, becomes a receptacle of vested interests, or is charged with meaning as a vehicle of personal satisfaction or aspiration" (1992, 233). Such a social form, because of this "distinctive character," endures, lasts longer, than the more transitory organizations or practices not thought of as institutions. Thus, longevity and the weight of importance people attach to its values are key distinctions between an institution and other forms of human organization. As Selznick put it, "the more settled the practice, the more firmly vested the interests, the more values at stake, the more sense it makes to speak of 'an institution'" (1992, 233).

Anthony Giddens emphasized time and distance in the process of changing institutions. In his theory of "structuration," the practices of knowledgeable human actors create the structures of social systems. Practices with "the greatest time-space extension" (those that are found in the most places over the longest time) are those that "can be referred to as institutions" (1984, 17). For Giddens, institutions are not permanent and separate from human intent and action, they are a constantly changing result of the things that people do.

So it appears that institutions are not inflexible, concrete realities outside of human control and beyond the influence of changes in their environment. Instead, they are the result of choices made by many people over long periods of time. If this is true, we are not helpless as we deal with institutions. It makes no sense to observe an institution and say, "We must behave as all have behaved in the past in regard to this institution, because that's how it is." We have the option of changing our relationship to institutions and of working to change the institutions themselves. Recognizing the possibility of change does not diminish the importance of institutions to human activity. Nor does it mean that we in the public sphere should act as if we did not care about past institutional practice and for the accumulated experience of other people in other times and places that has created the "institution."

In applying the concept of the institution to American communities, we could examine either organizations or practices. For example, an organizational definition could include all local governmental jurisdictions or identify each organizational type as an institution (cities, counties, special districts). Practices could be defined as institutions as well. Certainly, local police service is an institution, as is provision of local streets. However, to the extent that specific organizational types or service-based practices are defined as institutions, there will be marginal calls and problems with how to treat organizations or services that do not meet the Selznick–Giddens tests of institutionalism. Are regional park and recreation districts institutions? Are local animal control or health inspection of restaurants practices that should be defined as institutions?

It makes sense to define all local organizations and practices of public governance as "the institution of U.S. local government." Within this definition are found a variety of institutionalized organizations and practices, as well as organizations and practices that are not often thought of as institutions in themselves, but are practices of the broader institution of local government. Though the ideas in this book are applicable across the great variety of local governmental organizations, it is common in such research to focus on cities rather than other forms of local government, and this book is no exception. In their development over several centuries, towns and cities reflect the desires of Americans as they come together to create a vision of how to live together as a community. Thus, the focus here is on "the institution of American community governance," which may be thought of as a subset of the larger institution of local government.

As you read about the way American local government developed and the nature of community power in the rest of this chapter, you might think about the principles of Community Governance from Chapter 1 (scale, democracy, accountability, and rationality). What is the impact of the history of communities and the characteristics of local political and economic power on these principles?

The Separate Path of Local Government

It is common to mix the history and structure of American communities with that of the national government as if they were the same, but the values, stages of development, and the resulting structures are very different. The second theme of the book, the usefulness of the history of community governance in shaping the communities of the twenty-first century, points us toward events and issues little known by most people. Though elementary and high schools teach students about the history of our national government—albeit in a rather cursory manner—they teach little about the local level of government (Massialas 1990).

This is unfortunate, because this is a level of government that has been and remains crucial in the lives of Americans. The events of the eras of community governance help explain where we are today, what services we expect from local government, why we have the governmental structures we do, who exerts the greatest power and control in communities, and what roles we expect citizens, elected representatives, and practitioners to play.

The history of the institution of community governance can be divided into sections in any number of ways. I have chosen to split it into four eras that correspond roughly with centuries, beginning in the colonial period.

The Era of Elite Control

To understand the development of the institution of community governance, we may separate the institutional history into four broad eras that roughly coincide with the boundaries between centuries. The characteristics of these eras are cumulative—that is, new characteristics were added with time. So, though each era is given a name characterizing a primary feature of the institution of community governance during that time period, the name reflects an important addition to the nature of communities, not a complete shift or abandonment of earlier features.

The first era, roughly coincident with the seventeenth and eighteenth centuries, may be called the era of *elite control*. Early incorporations of many colonial American towns and cities were based on the English model of the borough, a corporate entity formed by prominent local landowners on grant of a charter from the crown. In the American colonies, charters were granted, and sometimes revoked, by colonial governors and assemblies. The English practice of the *close corporation*, in which the local notables who were granted the charter and governed the community also chose their replacements from among their ranks, was replicated in a portion of the new colonial incorporations, though this practice faded with time. In similar fashion, county government in many of the colonies was characterized by rule by appointed magistrates (Griffith 1938, 1: 191), though there were geographic variations. For example, Pennsylvania began its county form of government with commissioners chosen by the people (Martin 1993, 5).

Though most communities were not of the close corporation type, leaders who served on governing bodies were often wealthy citizens. Griffith noted the example of the borough of Bristol, Pennsylvania, in the mid-eighteenth century, in which five of the ten wealthiest men were members of the common council and were a majority of its nine members. Only one council member had an income below the community's 60th percentile (Griffith 1938, 1: 189–90). This situation was apparently typical of the "prevailing deference" granted those of the upper economic classes in colonial American communities, where "acceptance of a stratified society" was "the normal state of affairs" (Griffith 1938, 1: 189).

Circumstances were somewhat different in the New England "covenanted" communities in which people formed a town (likely to be, initially, a geographic area including several farms, rather than an urbanized center) based on a common commitment to religious standards of behavior. In contrast to "cumulative" communities that were formed of diverse individuals with a variety of interests, covenanted towns were "composed of individuals bound in a special compact with God and with each other. . . . This community, so covenanted, was the unique creation of New England Puritanism" (Smith 1966, 6). Such a community was a "Christian Utopian Closed Corporate Community" (Lockridge 1970/1985, 16), allowing citizenship only to others dedicated to exactly the same principles as the town's founders. In Dedham, Massachusetts, these principles included everlasting love, exclusion of the "contrary minded," mediation of differences by members of the town, obedience to town policies, and obligation of successors to the town's principles, in perpetuity (Lockridge 1970/1985, 4–7).

There were differences in founding circumstances between cumulative and covenanted communities, but the covenanted towns were initially, like the others, governed by an elite—in their case an elite of religious leadership. In Dedham, as in many similar towns, the pressures of population growth, religious differences, and attractions of economic opportunity in distant urban or frontier areas led to a gradual breakdown of elite control. The eighteenth century brought an increasing trend toward active policy debate and decision making by the collected members of the town meeting instead of the familiar deference to the wisdom of the selectmen chosen as town leaders. Over time, members of the town meeting took control by appointing ad hoc committees, investigating expenses of the selectmen, approving tax rates, and so on (Lockridge 1970/1985, 119–80).

However, even as the town moved slowly away from its original "monolithic corporate quietism" (Lockridge 1970/1985, 136) toward broader participation of citizens in town governance, the selectmen "still came for the most part from among the most wealthy quarter of the townsmen" and exercised considerable leadership in town affairs (Lockridge 1970/1985, 126). In fact, loosening of political consensus occurred simultaneously with, in the eighteenth century, increasing stratification by wealth in many New England communities. People of all economic classes served in leadership roles, but the relatively better-off predominated, partly because they had the ability to serve in the variety of largely unpaid and often time-consuming volunteer roles of town affairs (Cook 1976, 63–94). Also, consensus and religious conformity remained a factor. Zuckerman, who argued that eighteenth-century New England towns exhibited little or no control by elites, nevertheless wrote that

> a wide franchise could quite easily be ventured after a society that sought harmony had been made safe for such democracy. Most men could be allowed to vote precisely because so many men were never allowed entry to the town in the first place, because those who were there were of like minds. Indeed, within the compass of such conformity, extended participation ceased to be the danger it had been in England and became a source of strength. (1970, 187–8)

The Era of Democracy

The second era of the institution of community governance, roughly the nineteenth century, may be called the era of democracy, a time when "Jacksonian Democracy was the upsurge of a new generation of recently enfranchised voters" (Morison 1965, 423). This democratic tendency extended into localities, where Jackson's "populistic ideas had an important effect upon urban government" (Adrian and Griffith 1976, 2: 178). Beginning in the late eighteenth century and setting the stage for the democratizing changes to come, the structure of city government often was modeled on the new national government, with separation of powers between the council and the mayor and sometimes a bicameral legislative body.

In the nineteenth century, with the increasing size of population centers and the complexity of operating public services, city councils came to use committees of their members to administer specific functions (police, streets, etc.). However, the administrative burden was often too great, resulting in the adoption of the *board* system in which the council appointed citizens with knowledge or interest in a particular area to serve on a supervisory body. By the late nineteenth century, there was a growing perception that large legislative bodies and dispersed responsibility for administrative functions was creating inefficiency, lack of coordination, and the opportunity for corruption in the form of contracting kickbacks, patronage jobs, and direct payments to decision makers to ensure policy outcomes (Griffith 1974, 3: 53–96).

In the search for administrative efficiency, there were several experiments with the idea of having a council member be individually responsible for a department; in the early twentieth century this came to be called the *commission plan*, but it was tried earlier by several cities, including Nachitoches, Louisiana, in 1819, Sacramento in 1863, and New Orleans in 1870 (Adrian and Griffith 1976, 2: 161). From the 1880s to the end of the nineteenth century, the trend in the structure of city government was toward centralizing administrative power in the hands of a single elected official, the mayor, though not everyone thought this a wise idea. In his 1904 book, *City Government in the United States*, Frank Goodnow recognized the nationwide thrust toward concentrating executive power in a single person, whether in private industry, educational organizations, or government, but lamented the passing of the board system, which he found to exhibit the best blend of professional competence with public accountability (Goodnow 1904/1991, 189–200).

The Era of Professionalism

In relation to the institution of community governance, much of the twentieth century has been spent creating and implementing structural reforms to limit the possibilities of patronage, spoils, and control of government by political machines, reforms such as at-large elections to dilute the political impact of neighborhood (often ethnic) groups, and the council–manager plan, which uses the private corporation model of a professional general manager or chief executive officer accountable to a board of directors (in the public sector, the city council, or county commissioners). Such reforms work well where there is relative goal consensus and the challenges facing a community are largely physical and technical, such as challenges of infrastructure and finance. However, where the challenges relate to mediating or arbitrating between contending groups in the community, or when there are significant socioeconomic problems, the corporate model can be less effective (Williams and Adrian 1963).

The twentieth-century rush to professionalism accomplished what was intended, bringing to bear efficiency and economy to solve the largely technical concerns of rapidly growing urban areas. Almost one half of American communities today use the council–manager structure, although the "pure" manager plan has in many places been modified to include a directly elected mayor and often council-member election by districts. The emphasis on professionalism and merit-based hiring and promotion practices has been felt in cities with strong-mayor structures and counties as well. However, there has been substantial resistance to professionalism (Box 1993), with resulting movement toward mixed structural accommodations that allow a more politically acceptable blend of administrative rationality and political responsiveness (Box 1995c). The strong-mayor movement of the late nineteenth and early twentieth centuries is making a comeback, worrying the advocates of the professionalized city manager system and showing the strength of the citizen belief that government is out of the hands of the people who rightfully "own" it (Blodgett 1994; Gurwitt 1993a).

The Era of Citizen Governance

The name given here to a new era is speculative; to the extent that there is a new era, it is in the early stages and its outlines and future are as yet uncertain. However, it seems accurate to say that the era of professionalism is drawing to a close, and that, although the benefits of professionalism in community governance are clear, the reformist zeal generated in reaction to conditions in the nineteenth century has succeeded too well. A counterreaction to excessive bureaucratization and professionalization has set in, and this is a time of change, of movement back toward greater control by nonprofessionals, by citizens.

The contemporary challenge is not to achieve efficiency but to realize a community vision chosen and enacted by its residents, something that Lappe and Du Bois (1994) called "living democracy." Conceptually, this means a redefinition of the role of the citizen, from passive consumer of government services to active participant in governance (see Chapter 3). This redefinition requires that citizens take greater responsibility for determining the future of their communities.

The movement back toward local control and citizen self-governance has significant implications for the practice of public administration. If we are metaphorically coasting down the back side of the wave of reform that swept the early twentieth century—moving away from professionalism toward citizen control—then "traditional" public administration, based on administrative power, control, and a sense of positional "legitimacy," is a thing of the past. Naturally enough, there will be voices of protest with the passing of such a comforting model of what the public service practitioner should be doing on a daily basis, but it appears that it will indeed pass. This leaves the practitioner with serious problems to deal with, including how to make possible the desired citizen access in combination with an acceptable level of grounded rationality in policy making, how to avoid retribution from angry elites who see citizens and open dialogue as a threat to their interests, and how to prevent a return to spoils, patronage, and corruption, the evils professionalism was intended to eliminate.

The Institutional Legacy

Much has been learned about the institution of community governance over these four eras. At the beginning of the twentieth century, the thrust was toward efficiency and rooting out corruption and patronage, as well as toward solving the increasingly complex problems of an urbanizing society. Professionalism and centralized administration replaced a free-wheeling combination of democracy and machine politics. At the end of the twentieth century we are in a period of transition as earlier values of localism and citizen involvement in governance reassert themselves.

Today, the emphasis is on shifting the balance from centralized, expert-based systems to decentralized, citizen-centered systems. This shift is only possible because of the success of the reform impulse. If the battles for efficient and effective community government remained to be fought, if streets were muddy dirt tracks and water and sewer systems in their crude infancy, if local action was hampered by overly complex governance structures and administration was in the hands of political machines and their patronage employees, the contemporary discussion about citizen self-determination would seem trivial and foolish. Instead, we would be worried about solving the basic problems of service delivery, as were the reformers a century ago.

The eras of community governance outlined in the previous sections are indeed cumulative. This does not mean that we are always moving toward a more perfect future, but that we are accumulating valuable experience that can be used to deal with the problems of today. The era of control by a wealthy elite was superseded by democratic structures and processes, yet local government still had hierarchies and leaders, whether based on wealth or the power of the political machine. In the twentieth-century era of professionalism, many came to question the depoliticization of the community, the suppression of dissent and debate in favor of "unitary" goals of economic and physical development, yet the era also included broad opportunities for citizens to participate in local affairs.

As the twenty-first century approaches, the institution of community governance is a strong one, vibrant with value-laden controversies and containing a foundation of experience that allows for informed change. The lessons learned from centuries of practice are many and cannot be easily summarized, but I believe the institutional legacy includes two powerful, fundamental issues that are especially important today. The first is the question of the scope of local government, the question of what services local government should offer. Most people agree on services such as police and fire protection, streets, and water and sewer service (though even such basic services are sometimes offered by private residential associations in addition to governmental provision). However, it is more difficult to find agreement on a host of services that could be provided by the private sector but are often found in local government. These include items such as developing conference centers or housing projects, owning parking garages, hospitals, or golf courses, or providing ambulance, mass transit, or garbage collection services. In these areas, service provision by local government can compete with, or even preclude, provision by the private sector. Local provision of such services causes us to reflect on what we think is the proper model, in American local government, of the relationship of the public sector to the surrounding private market economy.

This question of the scope of local government also involves the degree to which government regulates private sector activities. Though we often think of regulation as the well-publicized actions of national organizations like the Environmental Protection Agency or the Food and Drug Administration, local government regulates a wide range of private activities, sometimes in concert with state or national agencies. These activities include the location and construction of buildings, streets, and utilities; who pays for provision of public streets and sewer and water systems; types of businesses that can locate in certain areas; the safety and cleanliness of public places like restaurants; the appearance of signs, billboards, landscaping, and building exteriors; provision of affordable housing; and many others. Different communities regulate such activities differently, and local debate about what to regulate and to what degree are often the source of heated controversy and changes in political and administrative leadership. The relationship of collective, governmental authority to private, individual behavior is a central theme in American history and in the history of the institution of community governance. People have strong feelings about it and are often willing to do battle in the arena of public discourse to have their way.

In this book, I spend little time on the substance of these matters, instead concentrating on the processes by which people reach decisions about them. This leads us to the second fundamental question growing out of the institutional legacy, the question of structural practices, or how to organize local government. In the history of community governance, people have expressed their values through the way they organize government. The desire for greater democracy led to the use of multiple boards and committees, the ward-based patronage system developed to allow for governance by political machines, and the desire for efficiency led to the centralized council–manager plan.

The structural practices question revolves around the opposing values of public responsiveness (fragmented systems, open citizen access to the policy-making process, organizational guidance by elected officials), and administrative rationality (centralized scientific-purposive systems, the citizen as outsider and consumer of services, professionalized decision making). The search for balance between these values is fraught with the hazards of a chaotic, inefficient, and possibly corrupt community on the one hand, and a coldly efficient, depoliticized, and bureaucratized community on the other. Decisions about where to locate on the continuum between these polar views must be made in a community political environment often dominated by an elite, sometimes well-organized and relatively hard to penetrate, sometimes loosely organized around issues and open to changing membership.

Structure is not everything, in the sense that organizations with the same structures can show very different operational characteristics depending on local combinations of personalities, economic circumstances, geographical setting, political history, demographics, and other factors. Even so, it cannot be denied that people believe structure and its associated practices are important. The four eras discussed previously each contain dominant ideas about the proper structure of local government. These ideas were a central, dynamic, living part of the goals community residents had for their attempts to create ideal communities. Within this area of belief in structure as an expression of community goals can be found commonalities of practice and points of contention, points at which the institution of community governance is changing to meet the new demands of the fourth era.

Commonalities in local public structures include the use of elected representatives of the people in place of the town meeting (though the town meeting is alive and well in some places; see Elder 1992); movement toward a directly elected mayor (though selection of the mayor by the rest of the governing body, a feature of the "pure" council–manager plan, is still in use); reintroduction of district elections or a mixture of at-large and district elections; professional administration of technical functions; and provision of basic services (though sometimes contracted or franchised) such as public safety, public health regulation, and the utilities/infrastructure functions of streets, water, sewer, waste removal, and drainage.

Points of structural contention include the appropriate role of the public professional, the strong-mayor versus council–manager debate, and efforts to increase citizen participation and control over decision making. This latter area is highlighted by criticism of overhead, or "loop" democracy, which is decision making by elected representatives instead of the people themselves (Fox and Miller 1995, 15–7). Concern about loop democracy leads to renewed interest in various forms of citizen participation, including use of committees, boards, and commissions to supervise governmental functions, thus injecting citizen influence directly into administration instead of routing it through elected officials.

In this book, it is assumed that the democracy principle is served if community residents are able to get information and make decisions about scope and structure if they wish to do so. This means that structure is very important, because it can hamper people who want to determine the future of their communities. For example, a local government with structures that block citizen self-determination might have some combination of these features: few opportunities for meaningful participation in decision making but instead meetings or hearings in which citizens are told what is happening and given a chance to give input; inconvenient public meeting times or long, confusing agendas and procedures; an overly professionalized internal decision-making process in which elected representatives appear to have few ideas of their own and almost always follow the lead of their full-time staff; and a complex bureaucratic system with lots of rules and little explanation. The scope of local government is an important issue, but in this book, the focus is on creating open and flexible structures and practices within the institution that will allow people to make their own decisions about scope and indeed about further structural change.

Such is the legacy of the institution of community governance at the end of the twentieth century. It includes concern about the following issues: localism (a preference for local as opposed to state or national decision making); citizen involvement and self-determination (making community governance open, accessible, and welcoming for those who wish to take part); demystification of professionalized systems; a desire to avoid the excesses of political intrusion into routine administration; a political environment in which elite groups are an important feature; an impressive technical–professional capacity; and lively debates about the scope and structure of community government. Let us turn now to an examination of the economic and political forces in the community that shape the institution and the practices of governance.

Power in the Community

It is remarkable how little we Americans know about our local government. We are surrounded by television and print media reports about national issues and events; people who pay attention to news and politics know about the president, the Congress, the Supreme Court, agencies of the national government, and issues being debated in Washington, D.C. News reports about state and local activities are given less attention and, even if people watch or read them, they often do not understand the political, structural, and economic contexts within which they occur.

Though most of us know something about how we came to have a national government with three branches, what each branch does, and how they "check and balance" one another—this knowledge may not be very broad or deep. Even graduate students in public administration may think that the act of creating the Constitution was a relatively placid event, a gathering of wise people who made a few technical changes to the existing government by consensus (it wasn't), or that there has always been a strong central government and general agreement that states are lower-level administrative subdivisions of secondary importance (not so).

However, this thin knowledge of the national government is more than what many people know about local government. Local government is the context of our everyday lives, the only level of government that has a constant impact on our physical and social environment. Despite this, even people studying for advanced degrees in fields related to public administration or working in the field frequently do not understand the basics of local government structure and function. They do not know why some cities have an elected person, the mayor, as their chief administrative officer and why some have an appointed official, the city manager (more than a few people do not know if this person is elected or appointed), or why many counties have neither, but instead a long list of elected and appointed officials with complex interrelationships.

Knowledge of the structures and processes of local government is necessary for citizens and professionals to choose wisely among the ways they may govern their communities, but it is not sufficient. It is not sufficient because it ignores the community as a whole. How can we decide what governmental structure to have, how much to tax the citizenry, or what services to offer if we have not studied our community, the socioeconomic characteristics of its citizens, the condition of its streets, housing, sewer and water systems, or what the majority of the citizens want for the future and how they view government's role in achieving that vision?

Value of the Past Number 1 reflects a growing desire for local control over the fate of the community, evidenced by local resistance to mandates and regulations from "higher" levels of government, citizen demands for a more open and accessible decision-making process, and calls for a "communitarian" approach to governance that emphasizes citizen responsibility for local affairs. The tendency for citizens to protest actions of local government, to complain rather than participate, or to object to changes in land uses (the NIMBY, or not-in-my-back-yard, syndrome) is viewed by some as evidence of citizen alienation from government. It may also be regarded as the first step in citizen participation; many people do not become involved in local governance until an issue close to home causes them to think seriously about their community. As they participate they come to understand the structure of government and local laws, the politics of individual and group interests, and what is needed for them to make a difference in community governance. Some people stop participating after taking part in the debate over a local issue, but single-issue involvement is for others a turning point at which they are drawn into local affairs.

Local control means that people in communities decide their futures relatively independently, putting outside pressures in perspective and fighting against closed or elitist political systems to chart a course grounded on a broad and democratic political foundation. This sounds logical and easy enough. People want to determine the fate of their communities, and they do not want to be blocked by national or state governments or by a few powerful people or special-interest groups. But logical or not, it is not easy. There are strong political and economic forces working against such citizen self-determination.

It makes little sense to examine local public governance in a vacuum, as if professionals and involved citizens could sit quietly in meeting rooms and make decisions about public policy without taking account of the community around them. The variety of community political and economic circumstances is so great as to be difficult to describe or understand in a comprehensive way. In a book about the "ecology" of local government policy making, Robert Waste (1989, 7) listed ten community features that affect the policy process: age of the community, locale, the growth process of the governing body, policy types, policy conflict levels, reform activity, regulatory activity, external factors, personality factors, and local political culture.

That is a lot to consider in trying to understand the workings of a local government. Despite this complexity, I present next some powerful and relatively straightforward ideas I have found to be especially useful among the many concepts available about community life, drawing them together into four community policy orientations that shape the environment of citizen and professional policy involvement. This narrative concentrates on models that broadly describe the political and economic nature of the community.

Running through the literature of community power and politics is the common theme of competition between communities for limited resources, competition that focuses on land speculation and development. In his book *City Limits*, Paul Peterson (1981) argued that the local community has limited control over the forces that affect its growth and development. This is because economic conditions are the result of regional, national, or global forces, national and state governments have cornered the policy market in matters of social welfare, and what remains to be dealt with locally is the use of land and buildings. Peterson wrote that, "Urban politics is above all the politics of land use, and it is easy to see why. Land is the factor of production over which cities exercise the greatest control" (1981, 25). Each community is in competition with others for whatever economic growth is available at a given point in time, so local leaders feel a sense of responsibility to promote development as a means to defend property values, jobs, and the condition of the physical infrastructure and the educational system, essential components of economic expansion.

Within communities, groups and individuals compete, attempting to use local government as a tool to gain advantage over each other. There are places and times when community life is characterized by consensus, cooperation, and gentle transitions, but this is the exception rather than the rule. More often, this is an environment of conflict, competition, and unsettling change— and this is not necessarily to be viewed as negative or abnormal but as the sign of a healthy democracy. As political scientist E. E. Schattschneider put it:

> Nothing attracts a crowd so quickly as a fight. Nothing is so contagious. Parliamentary debates, jury trials, town meetings, political campaigns, strikes, hearings, all have about them some of the exciting qualities of a fight; all produce dramatic spectacles that are almost irresistibly fascinating to people. At the root of all politics is the universal language of conflict.
>
> The central political fact in a free society is the tremendous contagiousness of conflict (1960/1975, 1–2).

How has awareness of the political nature of communities developed and what does it mean for local governance? Can citizens meaningfully influence the fate of their communities, or are they caught in the grip of forces beyond their control?

The Debate About Community Leadership

For decades, two opposing views of community leadership battled one another. The literature of urban power structures contains several notable milestones such Floyd Hunter's (1953) work in Atlanta in the early 1950s and Robert Dahl's (1961) study of

New Haven in the late 1950s. In the post-World War II period and into the 1970s, a debate raged between the *elite* theorists and the *pluralist* theorists. Elite theorists tended to use assumptions and research methods that yielded a portrait of communities as controlled by a relatively cohesive and closed socioeconomic class, whereas the pluralists used assumptions and research techniques that produced a view of community governance characterized by changing and accessible groups of people involved in specific issue areas such as education or redevelopment (Waste 1986, 13–25).

The debate between these opposing views became relatively fruitless by the 1970s. Both sides had recognized that a small percentage of community residents were involved in community governance, and they disagreed primarily on the question of a cohesive and closed versus fragmented and accessible leadership. In the 1970s and 1980s new ideas emerged to expand and renew the study of community politics. There are any number of ways to categorize these concepts. For example, Harrigan grouped them into five areas: neo-Marxist and structural approaches; growth machine theory; the unitary interest theory of Paul Peterson; the systemic power and regime paradigm theories of Clarence Stone; and the pluralist counterattack (Harrigan 1989, 191).

Bachrach and Baratz (1962) noted ways in which local elites could exclude the public from the governance process by keeping important issues from reaching the point of open discussion. They could do this by controlling the agenda of public discussion while making the really important decisions in quiet consensus among themselves; Bachrach and Baratz called this "nondecisionmaking." Verba and Nie (1972) explored the concept of *concurrence,* the degree of agreement about public issues between citizens and community leaders. They found that people of higher socioeconomic status participated more in community politics and community leaders were more responsive to them. It seems intuitively logical that political and economic elites would be dominant in shaping the community policy agenda, and research supports this assumption.

City Limits

Paul Peterson's book *City Limits* (1981) was noted previously for its emphasis on the community politics óf land speculation and development. Peterson argued that, as local decision makers make choices about policy, they do so in three broad areas: developmental policy, redistributive policy, and allocational policy (Peterson 1981, 41–46). Developmental policy is concerned with generating economic growth in the community, whether by luring businesses to the area, helping local firms to grow, or improving local public services like schools or infrastructure so the community is more attractive to businesses that need infrastructure to operate and schools to provide an educated workforce. Allocational policy is concerned with "housekeeping" functions such as police and fire protection and garbage collection. Such functions have relatively little impact on intercommunity competition, because most communities provide such services.

Redistributive policies "help the needy and unfortunate" (43) and detract from the overall objective of improving the economic health of the community. This is because public resources are used to assist less productive citizens instead of to promote the economic advancement of the community in relation to other communities. For this reason, Peterson argued that "the competition among local communities all but precludes a concern for redistribution" (38). Redistribution is seen as consisting of policies that are "not only unproductive but actually damage the city's economic position" (43).

According to Peterson, when the community successfully creates new wealth in the process of competing with its neighbors for economic growth, everyone in the community is made better off; entrepreneurs, owners, and managers benefit through greater return on their investments and they are able to employ more people and pay them well. In this way, a "unitary interest" is created in which the success of the governing group makes everyone better off, and all community residents share the same goals (interests).

The reader may notice a parallel between Peterson's theory and the debate in American national politics about "trickle-down economics." Peterson's unitary interest concept is much like trickle-down (supply-side) economic policy. Both hypothesize that the way to make everyone better off is to put more money into the hands of entrepreneurs, capitalists, who will then create jobs by investing in new businesses, production facilities, job training, and so on. Thus a decrease in taxes on the wealthy, funded in part by cutting social welfare expenditures, will theoretically result in economic betterment for all. The reader is left to make an individual judgment about whether this has worked on the national level. The point here is that Peterson's unitary theory is subject to the criticisms normally associated with trickle-down economics, especially that it may make some wealthy people even wealthier at the expense of some who have relatively little.

In addition, Peterson's theory has been criticized for being too absolute and mechanistic to accurately reflect the on-the-ground reality of local policy making. Robert Waste (1993) noted that communities sometimes do enact redistributive policies and that policies that appear to the residents of one city to redistribute wealth inappropriately from rich to poor, such as busing of school children to achieve better education of students of low socioeconomic status, might be viewed as developmental in another community, where a skilled and prosperous labor force is thought to be a good thing. Local politics are varied and complex, so that it is difficult to predict the responses of community residents to policy challenges. As Waste put it, "local conditions, local actors, local policyframers or policy entrepreneurs matter" (452).

The Growth Machine

Of the theories of community politics that emerged in the 1970s and 1980s, I find the *growth machine* model advanced by Harvey Molotch in 1976 and elaborated by Molotch and John Logan (1987) to be a good fit with the daily reality of local government. This model incorporates market forces, elite theory, the importance of land in the local economy, and the impact of non-decision making. It goes beyond describing the membership of leadership groups in the manner of elite and pluralist theorists in an attempt to identify the underlying mechanisms of community politics.

Molotch built on the idea that land is the dominant factor in local politics and economics. The basic premise is that the important players in community governance are those who have the most to gain or lose from changes in the rate of return from the use, development, and speculation in land. These people include those most immediately connected with land, such as landowners, local businesspeople, investors in locally owned financial institutions, lawyers, realtors, and so on, in addition to others who depend on growth for increases in their economic well-being (Molotch 1976, 314). *Growth* may mean development of vacant land or it may mean the improvement or redevelopment of land that is already being used. Not every community has significant amounts of vacant land that can be developed, but the effort to make money from the ownership and use of land can take several different forms.

Through their voluntary associations like the Chamber of Commerce and their efforts to influence the activities of local government, these people work to create a "we-feeling" of community, using athletic teams and community events to instill "a spirit of civic jingoism regarding the 'progress' of the locality" (Molotch 1976, 315). It is these leaders of community opinion and decision making who set the course of the city, and "the city is, for those who count, a growth machine" (Molotch 1976, 310).

In developing his model, Molotch took a relatively extreme, unicausal position about the linkage between the market-driven individual imperative to profit from the use of land and the nature of community leadership. The model assumes that, "People dreaming, planning, and organizing themselves to make money from property are the agents through which accumulation does its work at the level of the urban place" (Logan and Molotch 1987, 12). Because economic activity shapes community politics, Molotch finds that "this organized effort to affect the outcome of growth distribution is the essence of local government as a dynamic political force" (Molotch 1976, 313). The model is less concerned with the structural question of whether community leaders form a cohesive elite or shifting issue-based coalitions than with the underlying economic dynamic of urban politics. The desire to make money from land is pervasive at the local level. So is the impulse to use the financial and regulatory powers of local government to gain advantage for particular individuals and groups. The financial powers are those of taxation and debt issuance to build infrastructure; planning and zoning regulations are used to provide advantages to some people and deny them to others (Burns 1994, 54–7).

In a community in which the growth machine is operative, there will be people in favor of the machine's objectives and those who are opposed. Molotch's model is an elite model, because it depicts a strong difference of interests between those who benefit from growth and those whose interests might be damaged by it. Much like William's and Adrian's distinction in the section that follows between the work environment and living environment, Logan and Molotch contrast *exchange* values and *use* values (1987, 17–49). *Exchange values* are those of the marketplace, of people whose interest in land is primarily to make money from it. *Use values* are those of people whose primary interest in land is its use for creating a peaceful and pleasing living environment for themselves and their families.

There is a natural clash between these two sets of interests, because living space values may constrain those who wish to use the land for commercial enterprise, and marketplace values may threaten the living environment. It is for this reason that those involved in the growth machine attempt to control the agenda of community decision making, whether through influencing decision makers or keeping key growth-related issues off the public agenda (non-decision making). While the public is occupied with sports teams and other community events, the people who make decisions about and benefit from growth are holding a "dull round of meetings of water and sewer districts, bridge authorities, and industrial development bonding agencies" (Logan and

Molotch 1987, 64). Because these meetings are indeed dull and the decision process extends over months and years, few people other than those directly involved attend and the media pay little attention.

Community residents will come to meetings when a major decision point is reached, at least if it directly affects them. Sometimes people will organize to resist the growth machine, though it is difficult to do so on a sustained basis. There are places where resistance to the growth machine is prolonged and well organized. People may band together to protect their neighborhood from development they regard as damaging, local business people may resist commercial or industrial development that could detract from their businesses, affluent suburbs may resist development that might lower property values, and certain kinds of cities, like university towns, may contain groups of people who are highly active and vocal about the living environment.

Despite all this, the underlying concept of the growth machine model, that people naturally want to make money from the use of land, means that it is difficult for citizens to resist the growth machine phenomenon and that it takes sustained effort to do so. For public professionals, the pervasiveness of the growth machine sets clear limits to action, as the "growth machine elite" controls the political power in a community and thus can influence hiring and retention decisions affecting professional careers.

In recent years, many researchers have explored aspects of the growth machine hypothesis. They have found, for example, that growth machine elites use arts and cultural organizations to improve the market attractiveness of their properties (Whitt and Lammers 1991), that the growth machine phenomenon can be observed in established industrial cities such Flint, Michigan (Lord and Price 1992) as well as in newer, rapidly growing places, and that progrowth and antigrowth "entrepreneurs" may emerge to promote or discourage growth in a community (Schneider and Teske 1993a; 1993b). As with Peterson's theory, we need to take into account other political and economic factors, but it appears that the growth machine is indeed a powerful force shaping the environment of community governance.

Four Cities

Another way to describe communities is to examine the choices residents have made about the role of community government in local affairs. Oliver Williams and Charles Adrian, in their 1963 book, *Four Cities: A Study in Comparative Policy Making,* identified four basic orientations in communities; the first is a community in which the primary concern of the government is the promotion of economic growth. This concern in *promotion* cities is driven by "speculative hopes" (23) and a desire for increases in population and wealth. In such a community, "the merchant, the supplier, the banker, the editor, and the city bureaucrats see each new citizen as a potential customer, taxpayer, or contributor to the enlargement of his enterprise, and they form the first rank of the civic boosters" (24).

The second type of community is one in which the primary goal of government is to provide and secure life's amenities, the "home environment rather than the working environment" (25). In such places, growth is often seen as a threat to the living environment. Emphasizing values of the living environment as opposed to those of the work environment can be expensive, either in missed economic opportunities for residents or in provision of attractive physical facilities. *Amenities* communities tend to have relatively homogeneous populations—that is, their residents are sufficiently similar in socioeconomic status and desire for a certain type of community that agreement on community goals can be reached and kept. The well-to-do suburban enclave where people move when they wish to escape the problems of the central city is typical of this community type, as is the planned residential community developed privately within a city.

Williams and Adrian's third community type is one in which maintenance of traditional services is the primary goal of government. Residents of this *caretaker* city wish to keep taxes low, minimize land-use planning and other restrictions on the use of private property, depend on the "freedom and self-reliance of the individual" (27), and provide only basic and essential services through the local government. This laissez-faire approach to local government may leave the state or national government to solve problems the community wishes to avoid dealing with.

The fourth type of community is very diverse, with many interest groups competing for political advantage. The function of local government in this community type is to serve as *arbiter* between the competing groups. In this hyperpluralist environment the highest value is placed on political responsiveness.

Williams and Adrian found that promotion and amenities communities have "unitary," broad agreement on goals. In these places, centralized and professional structures such as the strong mayor or council–manager system work well. But in arbiter and caretaker communities, there is a pluralistic diversity of interests that is best served by decentralized structures that distribute power, such as the weak mayor form and ward elections for council members (29–31).

Williams and Adrian's typology of community orientations is similar to more recent work by Clarence Stone. Stone (1993) created a typology that included four types of communities as well. The first is the *maintenance regime* (similar to Williams and Adrian's caretaker community) that preserves the status quo and introduces few changes, and the second is the *development regime* that is "concerned primarily with changing land use in order to promote growth or counter decline" (18), much like the promotion community. The third regime type is the *middle-class progressive regime* that focuses on "such measures as environmental protection, historic preservation, affordable housing, the quality of design, affirmative action, and linkage funds for various social purposes" (19); this is analogous to the amenities community. Stone's fourth regime type is the *Regime Devoted to Lower-Class Opportunity Expansion*, through programs such as "enriched education and job training, improved transportation access, and enlarged opportunities for business and home ownership" (20). Stone sees this fourth type as being "largely hypothetical," though there are hints of it in certain places at certain times. It is different than Williams and Adrian's arbiter community, in which there are many competing interests, because the arbiter community may or may not emphasize a particular policy orientation, such as expansion of lower-class opportunity.

We might extend Williams and Adrian's work to speculate further about how professional administration is regarded in different communities. In the promotion and amenities communities where many people share the same goals and want government to play an active role in community life, professionalism may be especially valued. But where people wish to limit the role of government as they do in caretaker communities, or where political skills are needed as in the arbiter community, professional skills may be valued in the technical process of implementation but not in the process of policy formulation. Thus we may expect greater reliance on creative and innovative public administrators in the promotion and amenities communities and greater intrusion into administrative matters, with significant limits on administrative discretion, in the caretaker and arbiter communities.

The promotion community may encourage an administrative orientation toward adapting to rapid expansion, accommodating the needs of developers and business people, and showing a desire to "market" the community. Citizens in such a community may expect their public service practitioners to encourage innovation, activity, and change, although of a particular character. Where this is true, the administrative philosophy needs to include a willingness to find solutions that enable people to make money from land speculation and development, because the political environment may not be receptive to administrative action that puts aesthetics or environmental protection ahead of promotion and growth. Where political leaders come to see administrators as standing in the way of development, they may take action to decrease administrative discretion or move decision-making authority to higher levels, for example from a department head to a mayor or city manager.

In the amenities community, professionals in development-related services may be expected to be experienced in the areas of architectural review, historic preservation, requirements for developers to bear the lion's share of infrastructure costs, and regulations that protect the residential environment from the noise, traffic, and appearance of commercial and industrial land uses. With the greater emphasis on residential amenities, park and recreation professionals in the amenities community may have a clientele eager for attractive open spaces. The police department in such a community may focus on keeping residential areas free from disturbances and petty crime, perceived as largely perpetrated by outsiders.

Practitioners in the caretaker community may concentrate on cutting costs and finding new ways to do the same amount of work with fewer resources. They might be expected to support the concept of limited government, a limited sphere of discretion for administrators, and a minimum of change and innovation aside from that which saves money. Program or policy development skills may not be highly valued and administrators may be rewarded for keeping things on a quiet and even course.

The political environment in the hyperpluralist arbiter community might force administrators to be aware that most decisions or actions of significance will offend *someone*, given the range of competing interests. The practitioner might need to carefully evaluate her or his motivations and objectives, because public expectations and potential reactions to administrative action would often be unpredictable and may change from one day to the next. Technical, professional skills might be valued, but interpersonal and conflict resolution skills would also be very important.

Of course, care must be taken in applying such generalizations to a specific community. The four broad descriptions of communities used by Williams and Adrian may not explain some important differences between places. For example, though we might expect the caretaker city to be run by elected representatives who have a low opinion of professionals and government, it might be the case in a particular caretaker community that leaders value professional competence and administrative efficiency and at the same time hold to values of limiting the size and intrusiveness of government. Leaders in promotion communities might often care more for maximizing the profit of speculators and developers than for the aesthetics and environmental impact of development, but it is also possible to combine enthusiasm for growth with concern for amenities.

Two concerns common to communities in this model are the future of the community and the role of government in shaping that future. In local government there are a number of administrators who are involved in helping elected representatives make decisions about the future and the role of government. They include city or county managers, administrators and their assistants (where there is a city or county manager or administrator), and department heads and their subordinate professional staff in the areas of financial management, planning, public works ("public works" covers many functional areas, such as water, sewer, streets, airports, sometimes gas or electric services, and public buildings), parks, human services, police, fire, and others.

School districts face these questions as they grapple with issues such as whether to build new buildings or remodel old ones, where to expand and where to economize, and how to deal with calls for greater parental control or privatization of schools. Schools are not explicitly included in this narrative because they are usually administratively separate from general-purpose local governments (cities and counties) and are organized as single-purpose special districts. However, the concepts discussed in this book also apply to schools, as well as all manner of special-purpose districts (for example, districts that deal with air or water quality, libraries, parks and recreation, mass transit, animal control, etc.).

Though generalizations must be used cautiously and general concepts may prove inaccurate in specific situations, it is clear that there are important and identifiable differences in community orientation. For citizens and administrators directly involved in the debates over the future of communities or the role of government in shaping that future, differences in community types as described by Williams and Adrian may make a significant difference in how they choose to approach their work.

Varying Responses to Community Politics: A Case Study

Molotch and Peterson's models are subject to the criticism that they are based on only one thing, the response of community residents to pressures for economic growth, the use of the community's land such that individual (Molotch's model) or general (Peterson's model) wealth is maximized. Despite this potentially damaging criticism, the growth machine and unitary interest models have much to tell us about how community politics and power work.

Williams and Adrian's (and Stone's) typology of community values has the advantage of being based on contrasts between fundamental philosophical approaches to local government. In their typology there is no single issue that motivates local decision makers, but instead there is a general orientation toward achieving a certain kind of community, an orientation that develops over time as a result of the characteristics of community residents and their interactions. Some places are more interested in growth, some in balancing competing political interests, and so on.

These models are not necessarily contradictory. They provide different perspectives on community politics, politics that vary between cities and within the same city over time. I found this to be true during a research project in two Oregon cities in 1990. As described by the Molotch and Peterson models, land use was the most important issue in both communities, whereas each displayed characteristics that fit Williams and Adrian's typology as well. These two cities are about 10 miles apart geographically but worlds apart in orientation to community governance. City A was the largest in the region, a community of 50,000 that was the commercial and governmental center for the county. City B was a community of 16,000 that thrived on tourism, the arts, and higher education. Both communities were faced with substantial growth pressures during the study period, as well-to-do Californians and others seeking to escape urban centers migrated to Oregon. By comparison with California, prices for land and homes in Oregon were very low and the real-estate boom brought on by the new residents drove land prices up dramatically, making it hard for many long-time residents to pay their property taxes or buy a home. In City B, assessed property values had increased 25 percent in the year prior to my fieldwork.

The response to growth in City A had remained consistent over almost fifteen years, even though there were times when very little growth was occurring; in public meetings and in mayoral campaigns, there was a pattern of emphasizing growth as a good thing, a way to improve living standards for everyone and to provide jobs. City officials were aware of the need to manage growth to create a relatively pleasant living environment, one that could be served efficiently by city infrastructure. Even so, it had always been clear that citizens or professionals who asked uncomfortable questions about who benefited from growth and who paid for it were regarded as obstacles to be overcome and that growth was to be encouraged whenever possible.

Things were much different in City B over the same time period. In the 1970s and into the early 1980s, relatively conservative business people controlled public discussion of policies that affected land use. They were in favor of attracting development in much the same way as in City A. This was the case even though most members of the city council were, by the late 1970s, in favor of a more careful and restrictive policy toward growth. But by the mid- to late 1980s, the policy process had come to be dominated by a younger group. Though many of these people were also involved with the business community, most of them were concerned about preservation of what they saw as the character of the community in the face of pressures for change through development. By the time of my work in 1990, resistance to growth was not only a dominant value, the city council and planning commission had publicly and consciously decided that the normal market processes that determine the type and extent of growth in most places were not to be determinative in City B. Instead, decisions about growth would be made on the basis of impact on the aesthetics of the living environment.

Looking at what had taken place in these communities over the period studied, I came to realize that there is a continuum of responses to pressures for growth. In Williams and Adrian's typology, City A was and had been a promotion city throughout the period studied. City B had been a mixture of the caretaker and promotion types, welcoming growth but working to keep taxes and services to a minimum; then it changed to an amenities community. An interesting study by King and Harris (1989) examined attitudes toward growth of people serving on planning boards in rural towns in New York and Vermont. They found that boards in towns faced with growth pressures wanted to control or stop it through "rigid adherence to zoning bylaws and by reference to land suitability maps" (186). In places where little growth was occurring, the boards encouraged any potential development and approved almost any proposal. This characterization fit City B over the study period; when there was little growth the progrowth faction was in control, and with later rapid growth there was a transition to a strong growth resistance attitude.

However, this change did not occur immediately and the causes of the change were more complex than just the changes in external pressures for growth. For several years in the late 1970s and into the early 1980s the progrowth faction remained dominant even though they were no longer in the majority on the city council and growth pressures were increasing. Progrowth people were heavily represented on the planning commission and the people who spoke to decision makers on a regular basis about issues of development were to a large extent the business people who had a direct financial stake in the outcomes of the policy process. Because the economy had been poor in the mid-1970s, these people had not yet realized they could do even better financially by making the city's growth attitude appear environmentally sensitive, thus increasing demand for property and maintaining a strong rate of growth while property values went up.

This "conservative" group was largely replaced by new people in the 1980s. Some of the new decision makers were long-time residents (though relatively young, in their 30s and 40s), and some were people who had moved to the area in the last few years. These recent migrants tended to be from large urban areas to the south and they were often *drawbridge* advocates—that is, they had arrived, they liked the living environment, and they wanted to keep it the same by pulling up the metaphorical drawbridge to keep other people from coming to the community.

During debates on several proposed developments and during a key mayoral campaign in 1988, the faction that wished to discard the market as a guide to growth decisions became dominant in the policy process. So, in City B the change from active growth promotion to resistance took several years. External growth pressures set the stage for the change, but it took time for slow-growth advocates to build support, take over the mayor's position, and begin putting their people on the planning commission. The mayoral election was the point at which it became clear to everyone that the antigrowth sentiment that had been building in the community had come to political maturity and domination of the policy process.

As I thought about these two cities it seemed that the response to growth could be portrayed along a continuum that stretched from growth machine dominance to a weak growth machine. City A had a very strong, almost dominant growth machine; there were people who questioned the desirability of unlimited growth but they were few and far between. Specific projects would sometimes be challenged by people living in the immediate vicinity but development proposals would usually prevail in the political arena. City B had moved through a period of turmoil and conflict from support of growth to resistance to it. The growth machine in City B seemed virtually nonexistent at the time of my fieldwork given the proenvironment orientation of the mayor, council, and planning commission.

In between the dominant and weak polar opposites on the growth machine continuum are intermediate responses to growth. The idea of a dominant growth machine in full control of the governance process is similar to Williams and Adrian's promotion type, and it fits Peterson's description of the city with unitary interests. But it does not fit Molotch's description of the growth machine, which tries hard to convince people of the desirability of growth, distracts them with civic boosterism, and makes the crucial decisions quietly and unobtrusively. In Molotch's community the growth machine is vigorous but not dominant, so an intermediate step in the continuum from dominant to weak growth machine types could be called the *strong* growth machine community.

These descriptions of communities are really descriptions of local public opinion. A "community" cannot become a dominant, strong, or weak growth machine place; after we study and understand how the residents of a place feel about growth, we take an aggregate estimate of opinion and label the community on one of our continuum steps. What has been labeled is not the community as if a community could have a certain character separate from the attitudes of its residents. Instead, what has been labeled is our best guess about what the majority of residents would like to see happen with their community in the future. Residents form such opinions based on their past personal experience and their observations about what has been happening in the community.

City B passed through a stage of political conflict in the 1980s, from what appeared to be a strong growth machine community type to a weak growth machine type. During this conflict stage, community opinion was divided on growth issues with the opposing groups in some rough sort of balance; logically we could label a community like this a *conflict* type, adding it to the continuum between the weak and strong communities. There are any number of possible types of public opinion about growth that fall in between the weak, conflict, strong, and dominant types. Rather than clutter the model with lots of interesting but nonessential intermediate points, it may be better to highlight those public opinion characteristics that help us understand that differences exist between communities and in communities over time. The dominant and weak growth machine types are the extremes of community opinion about land use, the strong type is the community described by Molotch, and the conflict type, between the strong and weak types, reflects a community in which a lively debate is taking place about the future. The result is a four-part "expansion" of Molotch's growth machine model.

The growth machine phenomenon can take place in communities with physical room to grow and it can take place in communities with no vacant land through speculation, redevelopment, or intensification of the density of development. In addition, positive attitudes about growth are not only found in communities that are growing. In fact, some studies have shown that communities with little growth pressure are more likely than those experiencing significant growth to view growth favorably (Anglin 1990; King and Harris 1989). If this is true, it would be reasonable to expect to find places with stagnant or declining economies or population sizes in which the political climate is strongly progrowth. This makes sense, as people become concerned when the economy is bad and they worry about the living environment when the rate or amount of change creates obvious environmental impacts. For this reason, the impact of the growth machine on community politics and administration can be significant even where it seems unrelated to what is happening in the economic environment. A community in economic decline may be governed by people whose values are those of the growth machine.

There are a number of issues facing any community that do not seem to be directly connected with growth, such as how to treat questions of racial equity, whether to give public employees a large or small raise in the annual budget, or whether to build new parks. But issues like these are indeed affected by the community's economic situation. A community in good economic circumstances may be able to require developers to include affordable housing in their developments, operate a small business loan program in minority-dominated areas of town, attract top-quality employees with aggressive recruitment and high salaries, and improve on parks and open space amenities.

If Molotch is correct in believing that there is a linkage between the market for land and the content of local politics, the character of public opinion about developmental issues is very important to citizens and administrators. In the long term, the nature of land use and economic development has a significant impact on the needs and challenges the community faces. Choices made about who bears the costs of development and how private sector activity is regulated say much about the values of community residents and their government. Such choices constrain citizens and professional administrators in the daily work of making policy recommendations and carrying out policy directives.

Community Policy Orientations

In this chapter, we have examined the development of American communities, from early forms of governance to the current search for greater citizen self-determination. We have found that community elites often use the powers of local government, the ability to provide infrastructure and control the use of land, to benefit themselves. And, there is concern over whether this provides benefits for everyone in the community or transfers wealth from the poor to the rich and maximizes marketplace values at the expense of aesthetic values of the community as a living space.

The range of issues of importance to people in American communities is very large. This is not the place to discuss the content of the more common substantive issues or to take positions on how to deal with them. We must accord equal respect to all local interests and issues, focusing on the problem of enabling citizens to govern communities rather than the specific substantive concerns on the policy agenda of each community. In short, we are concerned with access and process, leaving issues such as economic development, race, income redistribution, how to fund streets, parks, and schools, and a host of other matters, to each local policy dialogue.

Even in the face of the complexity of substantive community issues, it is possible to distill into a few key points the features of community life that most affect the ability of citizens and practitioners to influence public policy. We have seen that visions of the future of the community and the role of local government in the community's future create a variety of political environments. Though a particular community is likely to be a mixture rather than a pure example of one of Williams and Adrian's four types of community orientation or one of the four types of community response to the growth machine in the "expanded" growth machine typology, there are very real differences in local political environments. The expectations of community residents and leaders about how citizens can become involved in the policy-making process and what role a professional administrator should play are important features of the local political setting.

In the dominant and strong growth machine communities, the conditions for citizen or professional action on policies affecting land and economic conditions are similar to those in Williams and Adrian's promotion city. There is significant flexibility and room for innovation as long as actions taken enhance the economic gains of local elites. In the conflict community there is a broad range of opinion about the future of the community, allowing citizens greater area for potential action. The public professional in the conflict community may find it difficult to take a position on a given issue without alienating individuals or groups because of deep divisions in community opinion. Paradoxically, failure to express a professional opinion or assist in policy formulation may also create an adverse public reaction. In this political setting it is understandable that some professionals may choose to keep their heads down, trying to avoid controversy.

Citizens and practitioners in a weak growth machine community are in a mirror-image of the situation of those in the dominant or strong machine community. They may have plenty of discretion to innovate but only where they conform to community values of protecting and enhancing the living, rather than the commercial, environment.

To the extent these ideas accurately portray community politics, the possibilities for successful citizen or professional action are shaped by attitudes toward economic expansion and the use of land to provide environmental amenities. This is not much different from Williams and Adrian's focus on the future of the community and the role of government in shaping that future. Or more precisely, the growth machine view of what is important in communities is a subset of the four cities typology, a part of the question of the future of the community. Williams and Adrian's typology adds the dimension of the appropriate role of government to the concern about land use. We can bring together many of the ideas from our discussion to this point in a four-part typology of community orientations to the creation and implementation of public policy. Each of the community policy orientations described next contains a continuum of thought (for example, from preference for a large role for government to a restricted role), so that the four orientations are not mutually exclusive.

1. *Accessible and Open or Excluding and Closed Governance System.* These opposing views of the degree to which citizens should be able to take part in the governance process correspond to the pluralist and elite views of community power. If a citizen who is not part of the "in-group" of powerful or wealthy people is able to enter the decision-making process and make a meaningful contribution, the governance process is open and membership in the governing "elite" is changeable and accessible to new members. If an interested citizen is kept on the fringes of the process, allowed to attend meetings but not to make a significant difference in local policy, the governance process is closed and the governing elite group is stable and difficult to penetrate. Becoming a member of this group or being trusted by them as an outsider may take years of volunteer involvement in community activities to demonstrate that the citizen is not a threat to the values and financial interests of the elite.

2. *Community as Marketplace or Community as Living Space.* This is a measure of the degree to which the local policy process is controlled by people who favor growth and economic development because they view the community as a marketplace, or those who favor environmental amenities because they view the community as a living space. A community that emphasizes the marketplace view may be one in which the growth machine is dominant or strong. One that emphasizes the living space view has a weak growth machine, and the conflict community lies in between, with polarized views of the desired future.

3. *A Desire for a Large or Restricted Role for Government.* This is the macro-level scope-of-government question. Those who favor a large role for government may have a variety of policy goals in mind, such as social welfare or racial equity, environmental enhancement, or providing incentives for economic development. Those who favor a limited role press for low levels of taxation and provision of only basic and essential public services.

4. *Acceptance of, or Resistance to, Public Professionalism.* This is a measure of community opinion about the appropriate extent of influence to be exerted by the professional knowledge and values of the public service practitioner. Highly politicized arbiter, or conservative caretaker, communities are wary of the influence of professionals, whereas communities with relatively consensual politics or those facing serious problems of finance or infrastructure may depend on professional knowledge. The degree of acceptance or resistance to professionalism may vary over time in a community, depending on circumstances and personalities.

Each of these policy orientations can have an impact on the principles of Citizen Governance. A closed governance system damages the democracy principle, resistance to professionalism could make it harder to fulfill the rationality principle, and so on. The ways in which community policy orientations affect the principles depends on the specific conditions in a community at a particular point in time. Taken together, the concepts discussed in this chapter and the community policy orientations supply the citizen, representative, and practitioner with tools for understanding the nature of community governance. In the next chapter, we turn to the role of the citizen in this environment to examine the options open to people who want to "make a difference" in their communities.

Three

Citizens

Models of
American Citizenship

In the beginning of the nation, there was little concern in America with what we now think of as organized citizen participation in government. We were a rural nation with a few urban settlements of some size and a number of small communities. Many citizens who wished to have an influence over community affairs could do so easily. The process of public decision making and implementation of "public policy" took place in what were, by modern standards, small and simple structures and settings.

This suited Thomas Jefferson, a deeply involved and fascinated observer of the development of the nation. Jefferson's ideas about governance were complex, exhibiting an interplay of concern with individual liberties and the need for citizens to take part in governance to create a viable community. The concern for protection of individual liberties from organized society in the form of government came from "the British liberalism of [seventeenth-century English philosopher] John Locke and related French Enlightenment ideas" (Sheldon 1993, 3). The philosophical movement called the *Enlightenment* was especially influential in the eighteenth century; it was a time of rebellion against established institutions, of "a self-conscious rejection of religion as the guiding authority in art, morals, politics, and scholarship." As a result, "a new spirit of critical inquiry, 'reason,' took religion's place" (L. C. McDonald 1968, 339). Enlightenment "liberalism" was not that of the large social-welfare state with which the word is associated today, but instead a liberalism in allowing individuals to make decisions based on their own reason and preferences rather than those of the church, monarch, or government.

Jefferson's use of Locke's liberal ideas, in particular the ideas that each person possesses a natural right to life, liberty, and property, and that government should be limited, was balanced with his concern for citizen involvement in governance. This concern was drawn from the classical republican tradition of citizenship originating in ancient Greece. Whereas liberalism emphasizes the individuality and independence of each person, republicanism views humans as social and political creatures with a desire to work together (Sheldon 1993, 8–10). According to Sheldon, "the primary components of this paradigm are that man's nature is essentially political, requiring an economically independent citizenry that participates directly in common rule, thereby developing and expressing its unique human nature and establishing and maintaining a virtuous republic" (1993, 6).

These ideas came together in Jefferson's scheme for governance in America, which included ensuring that each citizen owned at least 50 acres of land—in order to be economically independent—and a four-tiered pyramid of governmental structure: nation, state, county, and the ward-republic, a small sub-county unit. Each level of government would handle matters appropriate to it—for example, defense and foreign relations at the national level—but the ward-republic was the special feature of Jefferson's plan. At this level, every citizen would be afforded a "public space" in which to become involved in governance and to influence the course of community affairs (Matthews 1986, 77–87). People would feel free to voice their opinions, because their 50-acre farm would be sufficient to support their families and allow them to be free of dominance by the wealthy or powerful. Though Jefferson's ideas were not put into practice, they are indicative of some of the concepts of governance from the founding era.

Other people who influenced American thinking about the nature of government, such as Alexander Hamilton, emphasized greater strength, energy, and centralization of public authority in order to achieve effective governance. During the time leading up to drafting and adopting the Constitution, Federalists (in favor of a new, stronger government) and Anti-Federalists (worried that such a government would deprive citizens of self-determination) fought a war of words that the Federalists won with the adoption of the new Constitution. Americans had always wanted to prevent governmental oppression, but as they grappled with the problems of government before creation of the new Constitution, they saw a second dimension, that of protecting the government's ability to function properly from the self-interested behavior of citizens (F. McDonald 1985, 1–3). This led to the adoption of a Constitution designed to balance the values of democracy and stability, to allow for protection of individual rights and the ability to govern a large and diverse nation.

Jefferson recognized the need for a representative form of government at the national and state levels, but put his faith in direct participation at the level of the ward-republic. The Anti-Federalists wanted to keep governmental units as small as possible so they would be accountable to individual citizens who could take part directly, and they "accepted representation reluctantly, as a necessary device in a community where the people cannot assemble to do their common business" (Storing 1981, 43). In Europe, this worry about the antidemocratic tendencies of elected representatives was reflected in the work of the eighteenth-century French writer Jean Jacques Rousseau. In *On The Social Contract*, first published in 1762, Rousseau noted that "the waning of patriotism, the activity of private interest, the immenseness of States, conquests, the abuse of the government have led to the invention of using deputies or representatives of the people in the nation's assemblies" (Rousseau 1762/1978, 102). According to Rousseau this situation leads to dire consequences. These consequences may sound very modern to Americans today, with our national economy partially dependent on defense spending and deep public mistrust of the activities of our elected representatives:

> As soon as public service ceases to be the main business of the citizens, and they prefer to serve with their pocketbooks rather than with their persons, the State is already close to its ruin. Is it necessary to march to battle? They pay troops and stay home. Is it necessary to attend the council? They name deputies and stay home. By dint of laziness and money, they finally have soldiers to enslave the country and representatives to sell it. (Rousseau 1762/1978, 101–2)

The nature of American citizenship has been at issue throughout the nation's history. Sinopoli defined *civic virtue*, the basis of the classical republican model of citizenship, as "a disposition among citizens to engage in activities that support and maintain a just political order" (1992, 13). He argued that founding-era Americans writing as Anti-Federalists held a "weak republican" view of citizenship that included a commitment to civic participation as a good in itself, "not merely as a means of promoting interests and protecting rights" (1992, 11). Federalist writers, by contrast, were primarily occupied with the contractarian question of designing a governmental mechanism to serve the "liberal" Enlightenment concern with protection of individual rights, placing private interest over collective public interest.

The question of whether *liberalism* (an individualistic concern with protection of liberties) or *republicanism* (a collectivistic concern for the community good) is the appropriate model for American life is at the center of today's discussions about citizenship. Berkowitz (1995) suggested that liberalism is the dominant ideology in Western democracies and that the *communitarian critique* has provided a useful tempering of that tradition. According to communitarian theorist Amitai Etzioni, "strong rights entail strong responsibilities . . ." and, "we have a sound base of rights (although they need to be constantly and vigilantly guarded)." The problem is that "we have not matched our concern with the preservation of rights with a commitment to live up to our personal and social responsibilities" (1992).

For Etzioni, this means taking political positions that "shore up social responsibilities by shoring up value education in the family and by strengthening community bonds, which are the best carrier of moral commitments" (Etzioni 1992, 9). Specific applications include policies such as giving domestic-funding priority to programs that benefit children, changing welfare systems to encourage job training and avoiding unplanned pregnancy, and campaign reforms such as elimination of political action committees (Etzioni 1992). Etzioni has argued that communitarian action should be taken as part of the process of seeking balance between the classical republican and classical liberal models of citizenship. He wrote that

> Societies, like bicycles, teeter and need continuously to be pulled back to the center lest they lean too far toward anarchy or tyranny. The current legal and moral commitment to guaranteeing individual rights grew out of a concern about protecting persons from government excesses. The current commitment to advancing social responsibilities, on the other hand, reflects a concern that social institutions be properly nourished rather than abandoned. Because no society is ever perfectly balanced, communitarians seek to discern the direction a society is leaning at any one point in history and to cast their weight on the other side. (1995, 1)

On the liberal side of the debate, there is concern that in a communitarian society, people will feel intense pressure to conform to the norms of the majority, resulting in a bland, unimaginative sameness built on suppression of individuality and creativity. Writing of his observations of the America of the early part of the nineteenth century, French philosopher Alexis de Tocqueville believed that majority opinion stifled independent thought to the point that he knew of "no country in which, speaking generally, there is less independence of mind and true freedom of discussion than in America" (in Mayer 1969, 254–5). Tocqueville may have exaggerated the point, the early nineteenth century was a long time ago, and pressure to conform is typical of people anywhere. Nevertheless, in twentieth-century America there have been times when public pressure to conform to majority opinion was intense, such as the anti-Communist era of the 1950s and the Vietnam War era of the 1960s and 1970s.

There is also the danger that people who consciously differentiate themselves from others will view themselves as superior. Communitarians often base their model of citizenship on earlier societies in which citizens governed themselves, such as ancient Athens. However, the citizens who participated fully in self-governance in Athens were an elite of wealthy males, leaving women with few rights and slaves with none. In a critique of communitarianism, Derek Phillips cautioned that the human desire to differentiate one's group or community from others can be dangerous. As he examined historical examples, Phillips argued that

> movement toward the realization of community is frequently accompanied by feelings of dislike, contempt, and even hatred toward individuals and groups with different traditions, languages, religions, racial origins, values, and real or mythical histories and experiences. The examples of the Puritan settlements in early Boston, the German hometowns of the seventeenth and eighteenth centuries, classical Athens, those intentional communities studied by sociologists and historians, such groups as the Mennonites and Amish, and—above all—the ominous emphasis on das volk in Germany make it clear that hostility toward outsiders is often a consequence of differentiating one's own community from other groups. (1993, 165)

Today, the formation of gangs in urban areas and the chaotic and deadly circumstances in many areas of the former Soviet empire serve as reinforcement for Phillips's point.

Thus, as we consider the advantages and disadvantages of communitarianism and liberalism, it may not be a matter of choosing between one extreme and another—in this case between liberalism while ignoring the value of civic participation, or communitarianism while ignoring the need to protect the individual from the collectivity—but of finding a balance. We may be moving toward a balance in which liberals recognize the importance of citizen experience in the art of association to maintaining toleration and individual rights, and communitarians recognize that the practice of civic virtue rests within an essential liberal framework. This search for a point of balance reflects the constant tension between individualistic and collectivistic views of American citizenship. The moment-to-moment status of the balance tells us much about current public opinion on the appropriate relationship of citizens to their government and to each other.

The current trend in individualism versus collectivism in communities appears to be, at least in part, communitarian. Evidence for this includes the development of neighborhood citizen organizations and citizen advisory groups, not a new phenomenon, but one receiving new attention (Gurwitt 1992). This activity represents a redefinition of the role of the citizen, from passive consumer of governmental services to active player in creating a certain community character. The idea is for citizens to become part of their community's governance, taking responsibility for their local governments rather than treating them as something separate, either customers to be "served" or antagonists to be opposed (E. Ostrom 1993). The nature of this movement can be felt in this passage from Michael Joyce (1994) in which he described the contemporary American mood:

> They are sick and tired of supporting the bloated, corrupt, centralized bureaucracies into which our social therapists are organized to ensure that power and accountability flow to them, rather than to the citizens of the United States.

Americans are clearly willing and eager to seize control of their daily lives again—to make critical life choices for themselves based on their own common sense and folk wisdom, to assume once again the status of proud, independent, self-governing citizens intended for them by the Founders, and denied them by today's social service providers and bureaucracies. In short, Americans are ready for what might be called "a new citizenship," which will liberate and empower them (Joyce 1994, 7).

Hindy Lauer Schachter (1997) addressed this issue by contrasting two models of reform. One is the current model of *reinventing government*, a way of creating change through managerial technique. Using the Clinton administration's National Performance Review as an example, Schachter wrote that

> Current reform proposals do not include a wake-up call to the public to assume its obligations since customers have no obligations to the enterprise from which they buy products and services. Indeed, reinventing government's popularity may stem in part from the reassuring and complacent message it sends the American people. The National Performance Review implies that government's problems emanate solely from anachronistic legislation and bureaucratic procedures. Reform requires political figures to hustle and get their houses in order. Citizens can sit back comfortably in their rocking chairs and watch government improve to meet their expectations (90).

In contrast with this passive, managerial, consumerist model, Schachter described a model of "citizen owners" and "active citizenship" that was characteristic of the turn of the twentieth century and can be the focus of a revived citizenship today. This strong-citizen model leads to the conclusion that establishing an active public is essential to increasing agency effectiveness and responsiveness. *Active citizenship* is defined as people engaged in deliberation to influence public-sector decision making, animated, at least in part, by concern for the public interest, a concept that each individual may define in a different way. Active citizens shape the political agenda; they deliberate on the ends that governments should pursue as well as evaluating how well particular public-sector programs work now (1).

In applying these ideas about passive and active citizenship to contemporary community life, we may conceptualize citizenship along a continuum of desire to affect the local public policy process. At one end is the "freerider," a term taken from the economic study of public services. Economists use the term for those who receive for free a service others pay for. Here, it is used to mean a person who pays little attention to community affairs and allows others to do the work of citizenship, the work of studying and discussing issues and helping to make decisions about local public policy. The person who allows others to do this work for her or him is the "consumer" of public services.

At the other end of the continuum is the "activist," a person deeply involved in a variety of community issues and organizations. The activist cares about the community and wants to have a positive, lasting impact. In the middle is the "watchdog" who is attentive to community matters but becomes involved only on a few key issues of direct interest to him or her (Lowery, DeHoog, & Lyons, 1992, 76–7).

Freeriders and watchdogs sometimes think of the community in economic terms, as a "package of services" rather than as a center of personal identity, a home. If they are sufficiently upset with public policy actions taken by the community, they may leave it, moving to one that better matches their service preferences (Ostrom, Tiebout, and Warren 1961; Tiebout 1956). The question for the study and practice of citizenship seems not to be how to involve everyone in shaping their community, but how to make community governance open, accessible, and welcoming for those who wish to take part. Fox and Miller (1995, 36) noted that it is important to protect the right of the uninvolved to remain that way, lest in our search for active citizens we force them to be free, subjecting community residents to "the dead weight of conformity enforced by community elders."

Clearly, there are important questions embedded in these issues related to the principles of community governance. Structuring citizen involvement so that it is effective in shaping policy and satisfying to participants involves the scale and democracy principles in determining what geographic areas or programs a citizen body should deal with and how to make the process as open as possible. The accountability principle comes into play in ensuring tight linkage between citizen action and day-to-day implementation. The rationality principle asks us to include the expert knowledge of public service practitioners in the process and to urge that citizens take into account a full range of information and alternatives before making decisions. The following sections examine the social context of citizenship and ways to improve citizen access to the local public policy process in keeping with the principles. They also present the first of the three parts of the Citizen Governance model.

Critical Theory

The previous discussion begins in the founding era and ends with today's concern about the nature of citizenship. However, the contemporary situation is much different from that of the eighteenth and nineteenth centuries. To fully understand it, we need to think about the unique problems of citizenship in a society with a population of hundreds of millions, a complex economic system, and large organizations. Any major American city in the late twentieth century contains more people than did the entire United States of the founding era. From that time through much of the nineteenth century, to work for someone else in an "organization" was thought of as unusual, even unfortunate. The expectation was that people were independent, that working for someone else would only be a stepping-stone to self-support (D. Rodgers 1979, 30–64). Now, values of individualism echo in our popular culture (the heroes of movies with Western, spy, or other adventure themes are often loners pitted against the world) but the reality of most daily lives is that of work for an organization. We dream of being independent entrepreneurs, striking out on our own to create something new, exciting, and unique, but we respond to job advertisements asking for "team players" with excellent skills in "interpersonal relations."

Public administration theorists have given considerable thought to the impact of the societal changes of the twentieth century on citizens and public service practitioners. One interesting track in this thought has come from *critical theory*. The early critical theorists drew inspiration from intellectual resistance to German authoritarianism beginning in the 1920s. They saw the brutal behavior of the German state as symbolic of the oppressive nature of the modern technical–industrial civilization. This civilization is administered by huge public and private bureaucracies using a purposive–rational way of thinking that avoids examining reasons or consequences in order to focus on "getting the work done." In this view, modern Western societies turn the individual citizen into an administered cog in the machine of production, a unit who performs work for someone else and is expected to accept the status quo and be happy with his or her quota of consumer goods and leisure time in which to enjoy them. For the critical theorist, the majority is

> constantly bombarded with intensive advertising propaganda to show how well off they are and how fortunate they are to have all the things they have. They are trained to accept accelerating consumption as the inevitable way of their lives. And they are admonished at all times not to mess around with the horn of plenty because such actions will obliterate their jobs and their consumption potential. This is not a context from which militant masses, bent upon reform, are likely to arise. (Scott and Hart 1979, 219)

Long before critical theorists wrote about this situation, German sociologist Max Weber examined the growth of newly forming bureaucratic institutions and, as Ralph Hummel put it, he "recoiled from the bureaucratic future in horror" (1987, 1). Writing at the turn of the century, Weber "saw a strange new world in which not the brave but the dehumanized would survive" (Hummel 1987, 1–2).

The problem with all this, according to critical theorists, is that, "by virtue of its structure, purposive-rational action is the exercise of control" (Habermas 1970, 82), in itself a form of domination. Because the ideology of mass production, consumption, and the "good life" of material security becomes universal, people are unable to critically evaluate their circumstances and consider alternative ways of living. Though they strive to conform and achieve, they are left with a "vague malaise, free-floating dissatisfaction, irrational behavior patterns, etc.—in short, a situation of frustration and unhappiness which is not recognized for what it is" (Geuss 1981, 81).

Purposive–rational, task-oriented thinking is dominated by the elite experts and technicians leaders hire to direct organizational activities. Daniel Yankelovich (1991) wrote that when citizens come to accept the purposive–rational, task-oriented way of thinking as the only valid way, "then the deepest ideals of the founding fathers of the nation are betrayed" (240). This is because "when Thomas Jefferson enunciated the goal to base American democracy on an informed public, he used the term 'informed' as the Enlightenment understood it—to include thoughtfulness, ethical soundness, and good judgment as well as factual information" (245). Unfortunately, "we now teach young people to know about 'things'; we teach them forms of scientific knowledge. We do not teach them how to make choices with others. We do not develop the kind of intelligence needed to make public judgments" (242). The result is that today, we tend "to equate being well informed with having a lot of information," rather than with the older American, Jeffersonian vision of informed public judgment (245).

The trap of purposive–rational thinking, superficial happiness, and deep-seated malaise that does not reach conscious awareness is, to the critical theorist, a state of delusion called *false consciousness*. As a remedy, critical theorists advocate political action in which people are freed by giving them the knowledge needed to make their own choices. The desired "final state is one in which the agents are free of false consciousness—they have been enlightened . . . " and, "they have been emancipated" (Geuss 1981, 58). People resist this emancipation because knowledge of their true condition threatens their feeling of security, confronting them with the possibility of making choices that could be risky and unsettling.

The relationship of public administration and society can be, in the critical theory view, that of the caretaker of bureaucratic mass institutions for the political/economic elite that controls them. The public administrator becomes an agent of the very system that causes citizens to remain in a condition of false consciousness. This is not a flattering or optimistic view of the field of public administration—it invites the public professional to reevaluate whom he or she serves and for what purposes.

Governance by Citizens

The tension and balancing between individualistic and collectivistic views of American citizenship discussed previously exist within the modern social context of large corporate and governmental systems grown beyond the understanding of the individual. Though people naturally want to distinguish themselves from the masses to assert an individual identity, they know they must work cooperatively with many others to accomplish their goals. Americans have developed a system of rights and legal protections, yet they create evermore intrusive government programs to solve problems their grandparents would have thought to be entirely matters of individual responsibility. In this setting, how can we encourage fulfillment of the scale principle (solving collective problems at the level of government closest to citizens) and the democracy principle (making decisions based on free and open public information and discussion)?

A good place to start is by working to make it easier for citizens to participate in self-governance. How this should be done is an old and unresolved question. Arguing that in a modern mass society it is not possible to involve everyone in each decision, political scientist E. E. Schattschneider wrote in 1960 that the people need only express their opinions at key times on broad issues. There is no point to wishing for a complete return to a simpler world such as the world of the New England town meeting in which a large part of the population makes public decisions together. In the modern world, "democracy is like nearly everything else we do; it is a form of collaboration of ignorant people and experts" (Schattschneider 1975, 134). Therefore, "the emphasis is on the role of leadership and organization in a democracy, not on the spontaneous generation of something at the grass roots" (1975, 135).

However, in the 1980s and 1990s many people turned to just such spontaneous generation, attempting to create something at the grass-roots level. They were reacting against the passive view of citizens as consumers of public services rather than as people who decide what services will be offered and how they are delivered. Quoted in a *Governing* magazine article about communitarian principles in American communities, then Mayor Daniel Kemmis of Missoula, Montana, discussed the impact of the citizen-as-consumer model, saying that, "as long as we allow people to refer to themselves as 'taxpayers' and to think that their relationship to government is they pay the bills and get the service, then alienation will get steadily worse" (Gurwitt 1993b, 39). Wishing to take a more active role in public life than do the freerider or the watchdog, people may turn to a locally oriented, communitarian vision of citizenship because, as Christopher Lasch put it, "small communities are the classic locus of democracy—not because they are 'self-contained,' however, but simply because they allow everyone to take part in public debates" (1996, 171).

There has always been citizen involvement of some sort at the local level. In 1918, Mary Parker Follett wrote of the beneficial effects of neighborhood organizations as a way for people to experience direct human association in the urban environment. This re-creation in the urban setting of the communal life of the small town was, to Follett, the bottom-up key to creating strong cities. She wrote, "We can never reform American politics from above, by reform associations, by charters and schemes of government. Our political forms will have no vitality unless our political life is so organized that it shall be based primarily and fundamentally on spontaneous association" (202). In the period 1907 to 1930, people organized around neighborhood schools in the *community center movement*. The intent was to bring people together to offer recreational programs, provide a place to discuss issues of the day, coordinate social service delivery, train neighborhood workers, and counteract the perceived negative effects of less reputable gathering places like pool halls and bars (Fisher 1981). Today, local and neighborhood activity is often regarded as a means to improve education, citizenship, and families, and to combat urban social decline (Eberly 1994).

The current renewed emphasis on local-level involvement follows an effort in the 1960s and 1970s by the national government to make citizen participation a requirement of many social welfare programs that channeled funds to local areas. This involvement was mandated in legislation and administrative regulations, placed there by people who believed that programs were sometimes insensitive to the needs of those they served and could be made more effective with input from clients. Also in the 1960s and 1970s, citizens became more active in the process of planning the physical development of communities, in some areas taking a leadership role in creating and implementing long-term plans. Berry, Portney, and Thomson argued that, in the 1980s, the Reagan administration regarded citizen participation "as part of the liberal agenda it was elected to undo" (1993, 40), justifying "its actions by arguing that rather than trying to eliminate citizen participation, it was turning responsibility for it over to the states and cities" (41).

The traditional American suspicion toward government "gave way in the 1960s and 1970s to a deeper and more pervasive negativism" (Craig 1993, 2), beginning a trend of citizens reasserting direct control of the public policy process. Many citizen involvement efforts have been structured in a way that limits people to commenting on actions planned by professional administrators, but this is changing. In Oregon, for example, the state legislature passed a law in 1973 that made citizen involvement a mandatory part of all local planning efforts, and citizen involvement has become an integral part of governance in many Oregon communities. Nationwide, similar efforts have resulted in citizens becoming proactive initiators of community change rather than observers and critics. This can take the form of neighborhood associations, such as those in Cincinnati (Thomas 1986), formal review boards that supervise public agencies, or other involvement techniques, but whatever the format, it appears that the governed are taking a more active part in governance (Berry, Portney, and Thomson 1993).

In communities where there is a sense of agreement about the appropriate course for the future and about the role of government, there may be no reason for citizens or professionals to seek a change in the way the community is governed. But as we move into the twenty-first century, citizens may increasingly turn to local control of the policy process, demanding meaningful involvement and responsiveness on the part of local governments. In communities with differences in opinion between the economic elite and the general public, pressure builds for accessible and democratic community governance. An accessible and democratic system treats community residents as citizens, allowing open dialogue about policy issues and the ability to make recommendations or take actions that have real impact. A closed, elite-dominated system treats residents as an uninformed labor pool of consumers or as customers, using controlled public settings such as informational gatherings, public hearings, surveys and focus groups, ineffectual advisory committees, and so on, to manipulate public opinion.

In their book *Urban Fortunes*, Logan and Molotch urged communities to take intentional action to break free from the cycle of competition with other communities, to work toward a future in which each community assesses the impacts of development proposals, requiring people who would benefit to offset the costs to the community (1987, 292–6). Such requirements could relate to the physical environment (such as building and site design standards, improvements to surrounding streets, and transportation incentives for employees to use mass transit), to affordable housing (low or moderate income housing to be included in higher-priced developments), or to labor conditions (for example, requiring a percentage of new employees to be hired from the local area, training programs, or plant closure notification).

The desire to profit from the use of land is a pervasive local phenomenon, as is the impulse to use community politics and the coercive force of local government to seek advantage individually and for one's friends and associates (the "good ol' boy" phenomenon). Consistent opposition to the progrowth actions of community economic and political leaders is difficult to sustain, and sometimes difficult to justify. A primary purpose of cities in human society is to provide secure areas for commerce to thrive and we may expect people with the greatest financial investment in the community to work to protect and increase it. Citizen action that appears to endanger the economic condition of the community can be expected to draw powerful and persistent opposition from local elites, who may claim that citizens do not understand how the community works and that they are risking jobs and the future of the community with their radical and foolish behavior.

In a study of conflict between progrowth and antigrowth groups in Gainesville, Florida, Vogel and Swanson found progrowth people who regarded the antigrowth faction as "kooks" and "obstructionists" (1989, 75), people "unconcerned about the need for more jobs, opportunities for minorities, or the placement of an adequate infrastructure to support the population" (70). Antigrowth advocates were seen as wanting to "slam the gate closed" now that they were in the community, "doomsayers" who were "emotional, impractical, and uninformed" (70).

On the other side, antigrowth people in Gainesville often saw themselves not as opposing all growth but as opposing having current residents pay for the profits of the development community, and as bringing questions about growth into the open for public discussion. One antigrowth leader saw progrowth advocates as "greedy people," business leaders who believed that "if you don't wave the flag of progress every damn minute, city hall will collapse in economic ruin" (Vogel and Swanson 1989, 72).

One way out of the cycle of intercommunity competition and intracommunity factional conflict is through greater citizen involvement. Americans have become deeply skeptical about government's competence in delivering services and its honesty in dealing with citizens. Not everyone will be involved all the time, and many will choose to remain on the outside, either completely uninvolved or serving as occasional critics of their fellow citizens. Even so, many people choose to participate when given an opportunity to be a significant part of important change. For greater citizen involvement to occur, the community as a system of governance must be open to a free flow of information and dialogue between elected representatives, public service practitioners, interest groups, powerful citizens and the general public. This is a necessary precursor to finding a balance between living space and marketplace values, a balance favorable to the community as a living environment and the community as a healthy economic body.

Not all citizen involvement allows the same degree of self-determination, of real and meaningful governance by citizens. Ross and Levine (1996, 222–5) discussed a model of citizen participation created by Sherry R. Arnstein that portrays levels of self-determination. At one end of the scale, labeled *nonparticipation,* citizens are either manipulated into thinking they have real influence by serving on advisory bodies that have no power, or they are subjected to "therapy" in which they are led to believe that it is their behavior, not that of program managers, that is the problem. In the middle of the scale citizens are offered a *degree of tokenism*, ranging from being informed of agency decisions, to being consulted by means of surveys and meetings, to being placated with membership on advisory bodies in the midst of which they will be out-voted by people holding views preferred by those who appointed them. At the end of the scale where meaningful participation occurs, citizens may enter a partnership with the appointing body, they may be delegated power to make certain decisions and, at the end representing full self-governance, they are given full control over a program.

A common form of citizen involvement is the citizen commission or committee. Joseph Lee Rodgers distinguished between citizen commissions and committees. *Commissions* have legal standing in a community's laws or charter (the local "constitution") and substantial discretion, whether in making policy recommendations or serving as quasi-judicial bodies interpreting local laws as they apply to specific cases. Examples of commissions include "planning commissions; boards of adjustment; human rights and community relations commissions; environmental commissions; hospital, library, park, airport and utility boards; and housing and urban renewal boards" (Rodgers 1977, 10).

Citizen committees may serve in many of the same functional areas as commissions. They may be temporary or ongoing, but their roles are determined either by committee members themselves or by the authorities that create them, not by law or charter. Committees may be created in different ways, and Rodgers (1977, 12) identified these four (here paraphrased and modified somewhat): Individuals or groups may join together to work on an issue of common interest, such as health, crime, housing, and so on; the governing body of a general-purpose local government or special-purpose district may create a committee to give advice or to develop or administer a program; the community power structure may create a committee to study an issue or carry out a program, such as economic development; and a citizen interest group may form to deal with a specific problem or objective, such as promoting or opposing a proposed public or private development project, or creating and supporting a downtown beautification program.

Local elected representatives or community leaders may resist the creation and recognition of citizen committees, fearing that they will draw attention to plans and projects that community residents may oppose, thus costing leaders valuable time and money. Local public professionals may view citizen committees as a threat to their control of the policy formulation and implementation process, or as a drain on scarce staff resources. Nevertheless, the potential advantages of citizen committees are considerable. Among many such advantages, Rodgers (1977, 19–21) found that

- Use of citizen committees should increase public access to the decision-making process, thereby expanding interest in and understanding of public issues. This broadening of community knowledge should improve the ability of the community to equitably distribute power and public resources. Self-determinism in local affairs should be strengthened.

- Elected officials will tend to be more responsive to the electorate because citizen review of issues tends to improve deliberation, expand press coverage, and increase the number of alternatives that may be considered. This opening up of the process should reduce partisanship in decision making and expand official accountability, thereby increasing the possibilities of implementation once policies have been officially adopted.

- Citizen's committees serve as important vehicles for increasing minority involvement and leadership training in public issues. Many socially and economically disadvantaged people have been given their first chance to influence public policies affecting their neighborhoods through service on tenant's councils, project area committees, and neighborhood associations.

- A committee may establish a forum in which ideas and concepts can be tested and in which legitimate differences of opinion can be resolved. A general advisory committee often has been used as a mechanism through which representatives from competing factions can choose from several alternatives and agree on a single course of action.

- As an instrument for generating cooperation between private sector and public sector leaders, a committee may guide the use of private resources toward public purposes.

- Legitimacy may be given to local, state, and federal programs that might, without citizen committee input, lack credibility.

In many places, the citizen who enters the community dialogue about the future to effect a change in community policies faces a difficult and time-consuming task, one that may be unsettling and cause alienation from peers. Logan and Molotch noted that opposing the growth machine is not easy and that, "as the blunted careers of uncooperative politicians and the frustrations of thwarted environmentalists make clear, the opposition will be formidable . . . " (1987, 292–3).

At the same time, involvement in community affairs can be rewarding and satisfying. Rob Gurwitt (1992) reported on efforts in cities such as Dayton, Ohio; Portland, Oregon; and Minneapolis, Minnesota, to organize neighborhoods to deal with collective issues at the geographic level. He found increases in citizen interest in community affairs and a greater sense of community. He also found challenges in defining the roles of professionals and elected officials in relation to citizen groups, problems in balancing the interests of neighborhood organizations with neighborhood residents outside the organizations, and difficulties in balancing the interests of whole communities with those of neighborhood organizations.

For the public professional, asking community leaders to open the policy process to public inspection, dialogue, and decision making can be career-threatening, something that a person with a mortgage, family, and desire to advance in his or her profession may not want to undertake. I once talked with a city manager who had been in his job many years. He said of the business leaders in his community, in effect, that, "sooner or later, they will get me." Three years later, after a bitter controversy involving a few vocal downtown businesspeople, the manager left for another city and I talked to him about what had happened. He believed that this small but powerful clique of leaders saw themselves as being "above the law" and the manager as being "in the road" in relation to their plans to use city government's power over development controls to enrich themselves. The manager believed in fair and equal treatment for all, which required open discussion of public issues the elite wished to have taken care of in private (Box 1990, 195–6).

After trying and failing to change the form of government to a strong-mayor system that would favor the elite's interests, the city council hired a new manager who would conform to their wishes, staying out of policy making and assisting the elite when they wished to act out of public view. The new manager described to me his view of the role of staff in serving the city council as follows: "If there's not a law against it and they [the city council] want to burn down the town, our job is to give them matches" (Box 1990, 194).

For both the citizen and the professional, advocating widespread citizen awareness and participation can involve stepping between powerful people and their plans to use community politics for personal betterment. This sort of advocacy can be a significant act of courage. In the twenty-first century, the competing demands of the public for a say in local policy making and the community elite in controlling the policy agenda will contribute to the reshaping of the roles of citizens, representatives, and practitioners.

Barriers to Citizen Governance

There are formidable barriers to meaningful involvement by citizens in the creation and implementation of public policy. At the general, societal level, people often assume that professional government will perform tasks that in earlier times were performed by citizen volunteers. They have busy lives, they reason, and because government takes care of their public service needs adequately most of the time, they do not think of becoming involved beyond, possibly, the level of voting in community elections. As we have seen, there are signs that this is changing, though we should acknowledge that, realistically, only a relatively small portion of a community's citizens at any one time will become involved in shaping the future of the community. The problem is how to make it attractive for those who wish to participate to do so. In addition, there are several important barriers to citizen participation in governance that must be considered.

One barrier is the presence of politically or economically powerful people who resist citizen involvement as a potential threat. Another is the structure of representative democracy [or, to use Fox and Miller's description, "the representative democratic accountability feedback loop" (1995, 14), or *loop democracy*]. This basic structural format, used at all levels of American public governance, interposes elected officials between citizens and public service practitioners. It can help elites or interest groups to capture the power of public policy making for their own purposes, or simply to govern in ways that do not reflect what the public wants (or would want if given the information and opportunity to make their voices heard). Fox and Miller suggested that forms of direct citizen participation can be used to circumvent the loop problem, involving citizens, practitioners, and representatives in processes unfettered by traditional structures that hamper open discourse. (In Chapter 4, I discuss loop democracy in greater detail and propose changes in the role of elected governing bodies that would allow greater citizen self-determination.)

Let us imagine a community in which elected representatives sincerely want local residents to be a central part of policy creation and implementation. The question then becomes how to make this happen. As noted in the previous section, there are a variety of citizen involvement programs serving citizens who are "outside" the organizational structure of local government, such as those organized by neighborhood. And there are citizen committees and commissions that operate "inside" the governmental structure as a recognized part of the organizational hierarchy. Both are important, but here we need to focus especially on citizen involvement inside the organization. Outside programs can be grafted onto organizations that are not really receptive to citizen self-determination, but a local government that is structured to be governed from the inside out by citizens is a vehicle for real and lasting citizen control of community decision making. Thus, our focus is on the citizen commissions or committees

J. L. Rodgers identified in the situation where "a committee may be created by a local legislative body, public official or government agency to give advice, or to administer or develop programs for which the parent agency is responsible" (1977 12).

In our imaginary community with a governing body that wants to share governance with citizens, the traditional local government structure does not make it easy for most citizens to become an ongoing and useful part of decision making. Citizen advisory bodies such as the planning commission and parks and recreation commission are common, and there may be several others dealing with libraries, social services, review of architectural designs, building code appeals, or review of actions of the police department.

Though these opportunities for sharing in governance are valuable, they do not take us all the way to Citizen Governance. There are five reasons for this. First, some advisory bodies have little ability to make a significant difference in public policy either because they are granted a small area of responsibility or are given very little real authority, or both. Second, in many communities the opportunities to participate are limited because they occur only in a few functional areas (as with planning) and because some, such as architectural review boards, may require members to have specialized or professional knowledge. Third, advisory bodies, as with all citizen involvement structures (and elected representative bodies), may at times be dominated by a few people with a particular agenda. Fourth, the setting of public dialogue may not make citizens feel welcome to participate in self-governance. The New England town meeting is often referred to as the ideal of democratic participation and self-governance, a setting in which

> no one tells a Yankee how to vote, no one dictates; and only another Yankee can persuade. In a world where Democracy perishes, and in a country where self-government occupies every thinking mind, it is startling and refreshing to find New England Town Meeting alive and able and in the hands of a tight-fisted people who keep their heritage well. (Gould 1940, 10)

However, in a study of a New England town and its town meeting, Jane Mansbridge (1980) pointed out that direct, face-to-face dialogue is not always the best way for people to become involved in local governance. When people's goals and motivations are in harmony *(unitary democracy)*, face-to-face contact, such as that of the town meeting, can reinforce common purpose and friendship. But when there is disagreement and conflict *(adversary democracy)*, many people are intimidated and silenced by the thought of making fools of themselves in front of their neighbors or losing their temper and saying things they would later regret. As a result, some people avoid going to the town meeting, and some who go sit silently while the more forceful have their way (270–7).

Mansbridge suggested that direct, face-to-face dialogue may make more sense in unitary settings, although indirect forms of democracy such as referenda or representation may be better in adversary settings. The public hearing can be a good way to hear divergent views in an orderly fashion. It can also stifle dialogue as people come simply to argue for their point of view, to win by successfully influencing decision makers. In this situation, people do not really hear one another. Daniel Kemmis wrote that

> in fact, out of everything that happens at a public hearing—the speaking, the emoting, the efforts to persuade the decision maker, the presentation of facts—the one element that is almost totally lacking is anything that might be characterized as "public hearing." A visitor from another planet might reasonably expect that at a public hearing there would be a public, not only speaking to itself but also hearing itself. Public hearing, in this sense, would be part of an honest conversation which the public holds with itself. But that almost never happens (1990, 53).

Instead, public hearings are characterized by the formal procedural safeguards of due process, designed to protect individual rights rather than to foster community discourse. This may be a good thing in adversary settings where fact-gathering and legally correct decision making are the objectives, and it may be very wrong in unitary settings where reaching common ground is the objective.

The fifth reason typical citizen involvement structures present limited opportunities for self-governance has to do with the ability of citizens (or elected representatives or practitioners) to fully understand the services they oversee and to have an impact that is rational, constructive, and far-reaching. This can be difficult to achieve, because citizen opportunities for involvement in governance often consist of a small number of advisory bodies, bodies that oversee a wide range of complex activities so that there is insufficient time for citizens to understand the programs they supposedly oversee.

This is a serious problem, because in a very real way citizens are more than customers, they are the owners of the community and the services it offers. Public services are funded by taxes or fees charged to people using a service. Usually, the local governmental unit is the only provider of the service. In some cases (such as summer recreation programs) people can choose not to pay the fee or receive the service, but with many others (such as water and sewer) they have no choice. People who pay taxes cannot choose whether to pay them or not, and failure to do so has serious consequences (as may be discovered by those who fail to pay their property taxes).

Many public services, therefore, are monopolies financed through mandatory and coercive means. This is not a criticism; failure to coercively raise funds for services like local public safety or urban water supply produces outcomes most people find far more harmful than being forced to pay taxes. The point is that providing public services carries with it a crucial responsibility for direct accountability to the public. When people in a community collectively agree to tax each other so they can share the benefits of community life, each member of the community has a claim on determining how the community is run. Logically and morally, this claim is balanced by a duty to allow other members equal freedom and access to community decision making.

But public accountability fades if citizens who volunteer to participate in governing are not given a chance to make a meaningful contribution. The typical citizen "governor" on a governing body (such as a city council, board of county commissioners, school board, etc.), or a board, commission, or committee serves for a limited term and is a part-time volunteer, often called on to make important decisions or recommendations even if they do not clearly understand the workings of programs and cannot visualize the daily work of service delivery staff and its effects on citizens. There are many public professionals who answer to citizens only indirectly, though they may be responsible for a program with significant impacts on citizens and resources. Examples would include a utility department official in charge of a water system, a police administrator in charge of the daily operations of the patrol function, or a mid-level personnel manager in charge of labor relations. In a very small community the accountability linkage between citizens and service delivery may be preserved as practitioners answer to superiors who answer to elected representatives. These elected representatives have time and opportunity to become familiar with many of the community's services and are in frequent contact with many of the community's residents (as are practitioners).

As community size and complexity increase, elected representatives and upper-level practitioners only know the broad outlines of programs and services and they are in contact with a small fraction of community residents. Then, the accountability linkage breaks down because of the "information asymmetry" problem discussed by public choice theorists. The latitude of discretion for front-line practitioners expands as they control information that their superiors and citizen governors have little time to discover and understand. For practitioner accountability to a citizen body to exist, citizens must be able to judge professional actions and proposals intelligently and give effective feedback. For practitioners to feel accountable to citizen governing bodies, they must believe that citizens are capable of making rational judgments about program performance and have the time and desire to do so. If citizens interested in their communities are kept at the edges of a complex governmental system they cannot fully understand, all that is left of the accountability linkage between government and citizens is the relationship citizens have with elected officials, creating distance between citizens and public programs and taking us back to the problems of loop democracy.

The Individual
Knowledge Limit

All this seems to lead to the unresolvable, even depressing, situation in which local government operates without meaningful involvement and control by those who are its owners. Elected representatives have agendas that may not accord with those of the public at large, elected representatives and citizen advisory bodies do not have the time or knowledge to effectively supervise the operation of government, and practitioners, however benign their intentions, work in something of a public accountability vacuum. The accountability linkage has been broken (with violation of the accountability and rationality principles) and much of the problem is because of size. In communities and organizations that are small enough for people to keep track of the nature of daily work, those who want to participate in governance can do so effectively.

A way out of the dilemma of the broken accountability linkage may be to focus on the individual citizen or practitioner, examining what they are capable of knowing well and doing effectively, then building governance structures to fit this knowledge. The question of arranging organizations so that they can be effectively managed is not new. In 1937, in the *Papers on the Science of Administration,* Luther Gulick dealt with the concept of the "span of control," to Gulick a way of evaluating the number of subordinates a manager could supervise based on limits to the manager's knowledge, time, and energy (1992, 83–5). Gulick's discussion was not simplistic or mechanistic, but in a rather sophisticated way took into account the variability in span of control depending on differences in the sort of work being done and the characteristics of the workers. The point here is not to become mired in arguments about whether organizations can be structured "scientifically," but to explore practical ways of keeping the public accountability linkage intact. We can use a concept called the *individual knowledge limit* (IKL) to help us do this. It includes the five elements:

1. Measuring Success. A successful governmental program produces the greatest possible citizen satisfaction with the objectives, quality, and cost of the service.

2. Knowledge and Ability. If government programs are to be successful they must be governed by citizens and administered by practitioners who understand them in some detail. If programs are not governed by citizens who understand them and are committed to carrying out the public will, outcomes will be unpredictable in relation to community expectations. If programs are not administered by practitioners who understand them and know how to deliver the highest quality professional product, program outcomes will be unpredictable in relation to professional criteria of effectiveness and efficiency.

3. Citizen Understanding. For citizen governors (mayors, council members, county commissioners, appointed members of boards and commissions) to understand programs well enough to make informed policy decisions they must be generally familiar with the way programs work on a daily basis and with the more important technical and operational concerns. They must also be well versed in such policy-level issues as financing, evaluating success, and determining whether programs meet public expectations.

4. Practitioner Understanding. For practitioners to understand programs well enough to give competent professional guidance to daily operations, they must be familiar in a current and specific way with the daily workings of programs and the employees involved, including problems and issues surrounding personnel, budgeting, interface with the public, performance measurement using professional standards of practice and community goals, and so on. They must also be skilled in the techniques of management and supervision in the public sector to competently manage the people and resources involved in public programs.

5. *Span of Control.* For citizen governors and administrators to be individually knowledgeable about programs, they must oversee and administer only that range, size, and complexity of programs for which their level of involvement and time commitment allow them to maintain the necessary level of knowledge.

The individual knowledge limit demands that people who decide on policy or supervise public programs have knowledge based on personal involvement in both the policy and operational portions of the functions they oversee or administer. The level of detail of knowledge and decision making is different for citizen governors and public service practitioners, but the issues they confront are essentially the same in kind. Citizens and practitioners need to know about, at least in broad outline, the work done in public programs for which they are responsible, including, for example: programmatic/functional objectives; resources and financial constraints; the nature of practitioner positions and some of the people filling them; how the work is done on a daily basis; the effectiveness of implementation; and challenges and barriers to improvement.

When citizen governors and practitioners do their work within the individual knowledge limit, the practice of local government is considerably different. Local governmental structures are chosen, evaluated, and modified based on the limits of individual knowledge rather than uncritical use of conventional structures. There is much more dialogue between citizens and practitioners. There is less need for formal systems of control and reporting, and for constant reinvention of structures and programs to restore proper functioning. Also, the periodic upheaval experienced when mismanagement or inefficiency is discovered is much less common. Lack of dialogue, need for complex control systems, and periodic upheavals are to a large extent the result of an inadequate accountability linkage; structures created using the IKL restore that linkage and fulfill the accountability and rationality principles.

Creating Citizen
Governance

In today's complex society we cannot make all governance structures work as does the direct democracy of very small communities, but we can work to provide accountability and a sense of
excitement in self-governance. That is the goal of this, the first
part of the Citizen Governance model. This is not an easy task;
even in small communities, creating informed citizenship can be
difficult. For one thing, many people have strong opinions about
how the community is governed and how services are delivered,
even though they do not participate and their opinions have little
factual basis (such people are, in effect, misinformed watchdogs).
I served as the administrator of a town of about 3,000 people at a
time when we were preparing to ask the voters for an increase in
the city property tax base. The city council decided to split the
town into seven areas so they could visit each house on foot,
talking to residents about the upcoming vote. One day as the
mayor was going door-to-door, she encountered a woman who
had a somewhat negative view of city finances and how they
could be improved. The city was the headquarters for a large
rural school district with a property tax base more than four times
the size of the city's. Because the district offices and three schools
were a very visible part of the town's center, the woman's attention naturally focused on them, even though the district was a
completely separate governmental entity from the city. The voter
told the mayor that she would vote against a tax base increase
because we had all the teachers off each summer doing nothing.
We should put them to work all year, then we would not need
more money. Of course, the work schedule of teachers had nothing whatever to do with the city's need for more resources to
provide services such as street maintenance and police protection.

Such strong opinion and willingness to act on it despite any
real knowledge highlight the problems of citizenship and the

need for renewed efforts to make community governance as accessible and as attractive to people as possible. On the morning during which this was written, I heard a National Public Radio piece in which several people in Chicago were interviewed about voting. Like some of the Americans interviewed for the book *Habits of the Heart* by Robert Bellah and colleagues, some of the Chicago residents were interested only in local events and politics. They did not vote in national elections because the national level seemed too remote; as one man said, "What's in it for me?" This sounds much like the *Habits* interviewee whose sense of community attached to his direct surroundings. He said he had "a big problem identifying with hundreds of millions of whatever—people, flowers, cars, miles. I can see the community around me" (Bellah et al. 1985, 179). A desire to participate in collective affairs is most natural and easiest to cultivate when the focus is near and the results are apparent, as Alexander Hamilton noted in "Federalist Paper Number 17" in 1788, during the debate over ratification of the Constitution. Hamilton said that

> it is a known fact in human nature that its affections are commonly weak in proportion to the distance or diffusiveness of the object. Upon the same principle that a man is more attached to his family than to his neighborhood, to his neighborhood than to the community at large, the people of each State would be apt to feel a stronger bias towards their local governments than towards the government of the Union. (Rossiter 1961, 119)

To make community citizen self-governance accessible and attractive, we need to bring citizens in to the heart of the process of setting policy and administering community programs and services, and we need to create settings for participation that are open and welcoming rather than intimidating. Berry, Portney, and Thomson (1993) suggested that a good way to do this in large urban areas is through face-to-face participation in neighborhood organizations. This is an excellent idea for external citizen involvement and is a large part of creating an ethic of citizenship.

The focus in the next section is on participation within the local government organization, on internal citizen involvement.

Nineteenth-century democratic excesses (corruption, lack of coordinated operations, and control of finance and programs) in the use of service-specific citizen boards resulted in a shift away from decentralization to the centralized model of the strong mayor, then later the commission form, and still later the unitary corporate model of the council–manager plan. No one would advocate returning to the negative aspects of the use of citizen boards, but it may be that the reaction to abuse, the movement in the twentieth century toward professionalized centralization, has been excessive as well. Along with increased citizen participation outside the governmental unit, such as neighborhood associations, and changes in the roles of elected governing bodies and practitioners (see Chapters 4 and 5), I suggest that it is time to move back toward widespread oversight of community programs by citizen boards.

Use of citizen committees or commissions has an appeal based in the institutional history of democratic, citizen-based leadership of community government, but it has a firm basis as well in the practical mechanics of administration. For the democracy and accountability principles to be realized and the accountability linkage established, citizens must do more than vote for elected representatives, they must take part in shaping and reviewing implementation of policies, programs, and administrative procedures. In many smaller communities they do this now, and always have. Where they do not, the problem is generally one of size, of incremental disengagement of citizens from administration as systems become professionalized and hierarchical with growth.

Growth in systems and accompanying citizen disengagement means greater reliance on elected representatives to preserve some connection between community desires for public programs and what the government actually does. With time, increasing agency size, entrenchment of bureaucratic practices, and attitudes of practitioners toward citizen "intrusion," this connection can become remote and fuzzy. Reliance on elected representatives alone to actualize the will of the people can result in an uninformed and apathetic citizenry who only become interested in public affairs when evidence appears of serious deviation from what they expect of government.

Remedies for this situation, to have any real effect, need to be pragmatic and relate to the evolving nature of the institution of local governance. By themselves, measures such as increasing the level of discourse about policy options or decentralizing administrative structures are insufficient. They are not directly connected to the daily work of creating and implementing policy, nor are they grounded in the limitations of human capacity to understand and take action (the individual knowledge limit).

The difference between most citizen involvement structures in communities today and the one suggested is one of scope rather than of substance. Keeping in mind the individual knowledge limit, we can build a citizen involvement structure that satisfies the principles of Citizen Governance. In this structure, most community public service functions would have citizen boards participating in goal setting, policy making, and monitoring of administrative implementation. Each board would oversee only the number and size of functions its members could come to understand in a period of time reasonably related to their terms of office and the amount of time a volunteer could be expected to contribute. In a small community, for example, this might mean that one board would oversee the parks and recreation function, and in a large community there might be multiple boards covering the functions of park land acquisition and development, park maintenance, recreation programs, and others.

The degree of authority given each board, the means of selecting its members, terms of office, and so forth, would be matters for local discretion. The overall goal is interaction between citizens and administrators resulting in mutual trust and a perception of open discourse, sharing of information and values, and programs that successfully blend the benefits of the knowledge and experience of the practitioner with the desires of citizens. Boards can work well in concert with, and as a supplement to, neighborhood assemblies and other "outside" citizen involvement programs. They also get close to the real issue, the question of democratic self-governance. Unlike citizen participation structures designed to give citizens a chance to, from time to time, tell representatives or practitioners their concerns about government, boards give citizen members a direct and constant role in governance, an opportunity to learn the technical–rational aspects of public service and to apply them in real governance settings. Board members, as appointed volunteers who focus on a specific functional area, can empathize and take the time to talk to citizens who have concerns and a desire to improve their communities.

We often hear about the problem of micromanagement, in which elected representatives interfere in the practitioner's daily work of implementing public policy. Practitioners worried about this think they must resist citizen incursion into the provinces of administration because it allows nonrational political considerations to determine matters that should be decided only by professionals. The idea is that nonprofessionals should be involved only with broad matters of policy, not the specifics of how policy is carried out. This view can also be applied to the work of neighborhood citizen's organizations and to internal citizen boards. It is feared that interference by these groups could reduce the accountability of representatives to the broader public in policy making and degrade the rationality of administration.

The problem with preventing governing bodies or boards from engaging in what is thought to be micromanagement is that it is difficult to reach agreement on what micromanagement is and is not. It is not uncommon to hear professional administrators argue that any citizen involvement beyond very general review of program mission is micromanagement. Even such decisions as those about significant changes in the annual budget, procedures for hiring and firing senior personnel, and initiation of new programs or management systems can be seen by administrators as matters for independent professional decision. Some administrators view citizens as being insufficiently informed or skilled to make decisions on such issues.

The assumption that citizen knowledge of, and involvement in, administration of public programs is a bad thing ignores the individual knowledge limit and violates the democracy principle. It is true that governing bodies and citizen boards that submerge themselves in the daily details of program management, avoiding broader policy decisions, can damage program effectiveness. It is also true that citizens divorced from the realities of program administration cannot make rational decisions about policy. There are good reasons to see micromanagement as a positive rather than negative feature of local governance, and three such reasons are discussed below.

First, people do not routinely think in broad abstractions, they build conceptually upward from specifics. For example, practitioners may become irritated when representatives or board members initiate discussions about the details of purchasing equipment, motivating employees, or encouraging citizen involvement in service delivery. Practitioners may feel that these are matters of implementation that they should take care of and that citizens are engaging in micromanagement, specifying exactly what the staff should do when they are perfectly capable of doing it on their own. However, in discussing such details, citizens may actually be forming policies about the broader questions of agency relationships with the business community, the agency workforce, and the people the agency serves. Citizen body members probably do not know they are building policies piecemeal, and the product of such discussions may not (immediately, anyway) be formal written policies. But if they addressed broader questions without considering the details of daily practice, they would likely have trouble forming meaningful policies.

This incremental process is natural and logical. Sound decisions rest on a foundation of acquired knowledge and testing of ideas through a series of discussions and decisions. It is difficult enough for practitioners with plenty of information and experience to make logical, rational, and accurate one-time decisions on far-reaching and comprehensive matters. Expecting such abstract decision making of people who have been excluded from detailed knowledge and experience is unreasonable, and may lead to poor decisions and dissatisfaction with the decision-making process among those put into such a situation.

Second, public governing bodies and citizen boards often have divergent views and cannot agree on issues before them.

They represent the views of varied constituencies with interests that often conflict. Because of this, they may disagree not only on the details of delivering certain programs, but on fundamental questions of the role of government and over governmental actions involving direct impacts on people, businesses, and property.

Third, public governing bodies and boards have built-in incentives not to decide matters before them as general policy questions. Because elected officials, and to some extent citizens appointed to boards by elected officials, depend on pleasing individual constituents or groups to stay in office (Downs 1957), they are often hesitant to declare their position on broad questions of policy. Making a policy position clear in public involves the risk of alienating people whose votes are valued, and deciding isolated individual cases may alienate a few people or none. This being so, citizen governors often find it easier to decide a series of cases that relate to a policy position and that has the same cumulative effect as taking a policy position.

For these reasons citizens and representatives, short of becoming full-time professionals in the areas they govern, can acquire the knowledge needed for informed choice only by asking questions, challenging practitioner assumptions, debating with their peers and the public, and doing the difficult work necessary to make decisions about relatively minor issues within a broader policy area. This process of deliberation and accommodation naturally leads citizens into what some consider micromanagement. To ask citizens and representatives to avoid becoming involved in a series of detailed decision situations and instead to make a single overarching mission or policy decision is to push them into taking the risk of making a bad decision and of alienating constituents.

How communities are governed is important to everyone. We are in a time of significant change, a time of return to values of local control rather than state or national control and small and responsive government instead of large and bureaucratic government. In the twenty-first century, these values will mean that citizens will actively participate in the decision-making process to determine a vision of the community's future, the package of services the community will offer, and the governmental structures the community will use to achieve its vision.

These changes can be thought of as strange and threatening or as part of a seemingly natural cyclical swing in the relationship between the institutions of governance and the public. We are on the downslope of a wave of reform begun in the late nineteenth century, a wave that brought professional and rational administration to much of American local government but that is being modified by contemporary social and economic circumstances and a public desire to reassert control over the fate of communities.

In the foreseeable future, the process of moving toward citizen governance may help to revive earlier, enduring values of political responsiveness and democratic control, partially displacing more recent values of large government and professional control. This shift toward concepts contained in the scale, democracy, and accountability principles requires even greater attention to the rationality principle, as the temptation grows to cast aside thorough and balanced examination of information and alternatives in the rush to gain citizen approval of public policies. There could be significant impacts on the roles of citizens, as we have discussed in this chapter, and on the roles of elected representatives and public service practitioners, to which we turn in the next two chapters.

C H A P T E R

Four

Representatives

The Trustee and the Delegate

In 1774, English statesman Edmund Burke addressed a group of people who had helped elect him to Parliament, making clear that he would exercise independent judgment in representing them. He said that, though an elected representative should give full respect to the opinions of constituents and full attention to their business, the representative's

> unbiased opinion, his mature judgment, his enlightened con-
> science, he ought not to sacrifice to you, to any man, or to any
> set of men living. These he does not derive from your pleas-
> ure,—no, nor from the law and the Constitution. They are a trust
> from Providence, for the abuse of which he is deeply answer-
> able. Your representative owes you, not his industry only, but
> his judgment; and he betrays, instead of serving you, if he
> sacrifices it to your opinion. (in Hill 1976, 157)

This is a classic statement of the *trustee* view of representative service, in which elected officials interpret the public interest according to their conscience and judgment. On a continuum of the relationship between representatives and the public, the trustee is at one polar end, with the *delegate* at the other. Delegates see their role as discovering the public's wishes and carrying them out with as little interpretation or interference by the representative as possible.

Today, we often hear members of local governing bodies (as well as state and national-level legislators) discussing this question of the proper representative role. They want to preserve some freedom to act while appearing to remain in touch with the voters and sympathetic to their interests. The trustee role raises the *agency* question of whether representatives are doing what we, the public, want them to do as our agents. The delegate role raises the question of who the representative listens to in deciding what "the people" want. Discovering the public will is essentially a sampling problem—that is, a problem of accurately finding the opinion of the majority of the people on a particular issue.

In the small New England town of the past, representation was a less troublesome issue than it is in today's large urban areas. Citizens could attend town meetings and have their say. They had representatives, but they were regarded as temporary stewards of the will of the town, not as independent decision makers. If they deviated too much from the majority will they would be pulled into line or replaced because most everyone knew what they were doing on a daily basis. But now we have large local and regional organizations and representatives who can only know the desires of a few residents, unless they conduct an opinion poll. This is not a setting for informed two-way communication on public policy. In this situation, how can we recapture and maintain a sense of accountability, a linkage between citizen wishes and the actions of the governing body? This chapter explores ways to strengthen citizen governance by changing the nature of elected community representation.

The Nature of Community Representation

In Chapter 2, I outlined the history of the city council, a history of transition from domination by an elite in the early years of the Republic, to the excesses of democracy in the nineteenth century, to professional guidance in the twentieth century, and to the current search for more active involvement by citizens in governance. In 1969, Herbert Kaufman described the American discontent with representative government in a way that deserves quoting. "Opportunities for participation in political decisions are plentiful. Why, then, is there dissatisfaction with these arrangements?" He answered this question as follows:

> Fundamentally, because substantial (though minority) segments of the population apparently believe the political, economic, and social systems have not delivered to them fair—even minimally fair—shares of the system's benefits and rewards, and because they think they cannot win their appropriate shares in those benefits and rewards through the political institutions of the country as these are now constituted. These people are not mollified by assurances that the characteristics of the system thwarting them also thwart selfish and extremist interests; it appears to them that only the powerful get attention, and that the already powerful are helped by the system to deny influence to all who now lack it. Thus, the system itself, and not just evil men who abuse it, is discredited.
>
> At least three characteristics of the system contribute heavily to this impression on the part of the deprived: First, existing representative organs are capable of giving only quite general mandates to administrative agencies, yet it is in the day-to-day decisions and actions of officials and employees in the lower levels that individual citizens perceive the policies. There are often gross discrepancies between the promise of the programs (as construed by the populace to be served) and performance— sometimes because the expectations of the populace are unrealistically optimistic, sometimes because programs are impeded by difficulties that could not be foreseen, and sometimes because bureaucracies are too bound by habit or timidity to alter their customary behavior in any but the most modest ways.
>
> Second, the pluralistic nature of the political system provides abundant opportunities for vetoes by opponents of change. Each proposed innovation must run a gamut of obstacles, and ends as a product of bargains and compromises. So change usually comes slowly, by small advances, in bits and pieces. Those who regard particular problems as requiring urgent, immediate action are prone to condemn a system that behaves so "sluggishly."
>
> Third, the scale of organization in our society has grown so large that only through large-scale organization does it seem

possible to have a significant impact. This impression alone is enough to make individual people feel helplessly overwhelmed by huge, impersonal machines indifferent to their uniqueness and their humanity. In addition, however, some interests—notably those of Negroes and of youth—have recently begun to develop the organizational skills to mobilize their political resources only to find that it takes time to build channels of access to political structures. Rather than wait for admission to these structures—where, incidentally, they are likely to encounter larger, more experienced, well-entrenched organizations opposed to them—these groups, while continuing to strive for recognition in the older institutions, have adopted a strategy of deriding those institutions and seeking to build new ones in which they can have greater, perhaps dominant, influence.

Thus, the plenitude of traditional modes of representation no longer suffices; the existing methods do not adequately accommodate many of the demands upon them. Just as the adaptation of governmental design during the past century has gravitated toward furnishing expertise and leadership, so it is now under pressure from several quarters to accord a greater role to representativeness. (4–5)

Kaufman wrote more than a quarter of a century ago. The people he believed felt disenfranchised were minorities and the poor. Now, although these groups still face serious problems, a much wider spectrum of citizens believe that representative governmental structures are not doing what they should. For example, the International City/County Management Association (Frisby and Bowman 1996) reported the results of focus-group discussions with citizens in 1990 and 1991 about their failure to participate in the political process. The citizens felt that they had been denied access to the political process, that "no one is listening," that special interest groups and lobbyists control the policy process, and that "public officials pursue their own self-serving agendas, which have little to do with the common good" (A-1, A-2). Daniel Yankelovich wrote that most Americans "do not think that their contributions are wanted" and that "they are, of course, correct in this latter assumption: policy makers do not really seek public input" (1991, 244).

Some of this citizen dissatisfaction with representative government is directed at the national level and is part of the reason that citizens who wish to become involved in public life increasingly turn to the local level. However, the concern about representation extends to all levels of government. It is a concern about how small groups of elected people handle the complexity and pressure of responding to many voices as they make decisions about public programs and resources. It is a concern about how to handle the situation in which citizens come to believe that their representatives, whether members of Congress, a state legislature, or the local city council, county commissioners, or school board, fail to do what citizens think is right. This concern with failure to govern, at least as perceived by some segment of the population, is at the heart of efforts to change the relationship of citizens to governing bodies. It is at the heart of the problem of "loop democracy," in which citizens must express their will through representatives rather than by direct action.

At the time of the founding of the nation, people interested in creating a stronger national government believed that its powers must ultimately be derived from the people, but that most citizens lacked the ability to assume a constructive and active role in governing. The Founders believed that government, at least at the national level, should be run by philosophically minded people who, unlike the squabbling factional interests at the state level, would have the interests of the entire nation at heart. However, at the local level it was assumed that people govern themselves more or less directly, because of the geographic immediacy of the citizens, the activities of government, and the elected representatives.

In situations in which there is apparent failure of local representatives to govern in the interests of the majority of citizens, part of the problem, as discussed in Chapters 2 and 3, often relates to control of the governing body by an economic elite. Part of the problem may also involve the internal workings of governing bodies. Do they function cooperatively, thinking together about the overall problems facing their communities, working toward consensual programmatic solutions? Or are governing bodies a collection of people representing different economic, geographic, or political interests competing for a limited pool of resources? The cooperative model is the one advocated by reformers in the twentieth century. It is a model that views members of governing bodies as community-minded instead of self-interested and it contrasts with the competitive model, common through the nineteenth century and reemerging in the late twentieth century. This is a model of diversity of views, of conflict, and compromise.

The cooperative model encourages city councils to work together toward common goals that benefit the entire community. In this model, the governing body focuses on the task of setting the mission of the organization, responds thoughtfully to staff policy proposals, and avoids becoming involved in detailed issues of implementation (Svara 1986a). The mayor in the cooperative setting may serve as facilitator of communications, as an advocate for new policies, or as the visible center of community leadership (Svara 1986b). Mayors can exercise a meaningful leadership role in any structural format. Though they often would prefer to have the full executive authority of a strong mayor, it has been recognized for some time that mayors in council–manager cities can be effective as policy leaders (Sparrow 1985; Wikstrom 1979).

A competitive view of local governing bodies does not discount these functions of the governing body and mayor, but recognizes the potential for internal tension and discord. The cooperative model assumes that members of governing bodies seek to serve a general public interest. But by their representative nature, governing bodies are composed of people who may serve the specific interests of geographic areas, special interests, or personal gain in the form of exercise of power, a career in public elected life, or financial enrichment. The interests of individual governing body members are often at odds, causing lack of common direction in values or goals. Governing body members are usually not experts on governmental operations, and they lack the access practitioners have to technical information and the time to absorb it. Politically, they are inclined to avoid the risk of taking clear public stands on issues (White 1982), preferring to serve as critics of proposals from the staff or others (Adrian 1958). The need for political leadership and the direct election of mayors offers an opportunity for mayors to step forward as policy leaders, increasing the likelihood of conflict between mayors and governing bodies and making the relationship between the mayor and the governing body function much like the separation-of-powers structure at the state and national levels.

During the reform era in the first part of the twentieth century, it was assumed that a cooperative and consensual governing body that holds the entire community in view would produce public policies and programs in the public interest. But this assumption ignored the possibility that representatives might favor certain elites, or slight the needs of minorities, or pursue goals not preferred by the majority of citizens. This has led to a modest shift back to election of governing body members by geographic area rather than having everyone in the community vote on every member in "at-large" elections (Ross and Levine 1996, 187–9). The cooperative, community-wide reform model, it turns out, can have the same effect at the local level as the Founders intended by having an elite group of decision makers in the nation's capital—that is, removal of some the "politics" from local affairs. Though this may lead to better governance at the national level, locally it can lead to public resentment toward what appears to be a select group making decisions for their own benefit, removed from public accountability.

The Reform Era model of consensual, community-minded governing bodies and boards is appealing to those who would like local government to be reasonable, rational, and apolitical, but the reality of democratic governance is often the reality of division, debate, and conflict. This is not necessarily negative; it can be a reflection of the health of the democratic process. Indeed, a governing body that seems to be in agreement about most everything might be a signal that a community is being governed by people who are using the structure and power of government to advance their own interests.

The previous discussion outlines several ways in which representation can cause citizens to think that their interests are not being served. Procedurally, the size and complexity of government can leave people feeling unable to take part in governance to have their ideas heard. Substantively, they may believe that their taxes are too high, certain services are not delivered efficiently, land development proposals are being approved without consideration of the wishes of the public, certain neighborhoods are being ignored, public managers are arrogant and fond of red tape, public schools are deteriorating despite infusions of tax-generated funds, and so on. When there is poor "concurrence" (Verba and Nie 1972, 299–333) between public opinion about community issues and the opinions of representatives and their appointed professionals, the question of political failure arises.

Let us look at some characteristics of local governing bodies, starting with a refresher on the four basic community policy orientations discussed at the end of Chapter 2. Then we will move into assessing the capability of representative bodies to serve citizen needs by fulfilling the democracy, accountability, and rationality principles, concluding with the second part of the Citizen Governance model.

The Burden of Representation

When people observe what they think is poor representation in their community, they are often encountering, and reacting negatively to, one of the community policy orientations we have discussed. From Chapter 2, the reader will remember that these are an accessible and open or excluding and closed governance system; an emphasis on the community as marketplace or the community as living environment; a desire for a large or restricted role for government; and acceptance of, or resistance to, professionalism. A citizen who has a strongly held opinion on one or more of these policy orientations is likely to be unhappy with a governing body that disagrees with him or her.

These governing-body policy orientations relate to desired outcomes for the future of the community and to attitudes about citizens and practitioners. In addition to policy orientations, the people on a council or board each have a view of the appropriate role of the representative. The dominant view among them can be described along a continuum of governing body approach to representation, with the delegate and the trustee at the polar ends.

The delegate governing body is mostly concerned with correctly identifying what the majority of the people want, or at least the majority of those who take notice of governing body policy choices. Identifying this majority of the politically aware is a matter of sampling. What is the best way to discover public opinion? Talk to acquaintances, send out a survey, listen to coffee-shop talk, go door-to-door, read the letters to the editor of the newspaper, pay attention to the people who come to public hearings, or take part in neighborhood groups?

The trustee governing body seeks to identify what it considers to be policy in the public interest. This may mean the members' personal visions of the community's future, or it may be a sense of what the majority of the people would want if they were well informed and active in community affairs. The trustee governing body is wary of acting on the opinions of people with a vested interest in certain policy positions. They also may actively work to shape public opinion.

In between the delegate and the trustee governing body on this continuum of representation is the group that shares an interest in advocating a particular policy orientation. This "advocate" governing body may show an inclination toward a position on one of the policy orientations discussed previously or some other, but the observer will, over time, notice a special interest in promoting a policy, outcome, or attitude toward citizens or practitioners. For example, it is not uncommon to find a governing body that promotes economic development or environmental protection, or a body that discounts or is very deferential to career practitioners. Over time in a given community, the observer might note changes in the policy orientation theme as new bodies are formed following elections. It is this mixture of policy orientation and approach to representation that produces the rich and complex range of governing body behaviors in local communities. Though care should be exercised in "typing" a governing body using the four policy orientations and the trustee–delegate continuum of representation, the purpose of gaining a greater understanding of governing body behavior is to find improved ways of governing.

To this point in the book, we have discussed important features of local representation and we have identified some concerns about representation that can be summarized as follows:

1. *Elite Group Control of the Public Policy Process.* As discussed in Chapter 2, this is the problem of which interests tend to dominate the local public policy process. It is the problem of "who benefits and who pays" that is common to much human activity.

2. *Loop Democracy.* This is the question of whether citizen wishes for community governance should be "filtered" through elected representatives and whether the interests of these elected officials change the result of the public policy process to something different than the desires of the majority of citizens.

3. *Individual Knowledge.* Elected representatives do not generally have the time nor expertise to oversee, supervise, and make rational decisions about the conduct of public programs. This is the problem addressed by the individual knowledge limit in Chapter 3. It can result in crisis decision making when, because of this lack of knowledge, the accountability linkage between citizen preferences and the delivery of public services is broken. At periodic intervals, a few of the more serious problems caused by this lack of accountability rise to the level of awareness by governing bodies, resulting in sporadic, crisis-driven efforts to fix a government that appears to be "broken," out of control.

From the viewpoint of the citizen or the practitioner, failure of representation occurs when the policy orientation or the approach to representation of the governing body is at odds with the will of the majority of citizens ("majority" in the sense of that number of citizens with knowledge of events and desire to become involved in community affairs). This is essentially a problem of agency, a useful concept in thinking about the accountability linkages between citizens, representatives, and practitioners.

If one person decides to perform certain work on his or her own, there is no accountability problem, no problem in determining whether the person is doing what he or she wants to have done. But when that person hires an employee to assist in the work, an agency problem develops. Kathleen Eisenhardt wrote that agency theory, grounded in the intellectual assumptions of the discipline of economics, deals with "the ubiquitous agency relationship, in which one party (the principal) delegates work to another (the agent) who performs that work." According to Eisenhardt, one of the central questions dealt with in agency theory is the situation "that arises when (a) the desires or goals of the principal and agent conflict and (b) it is difficult or expensive for the principal to verify what the agent is actually doing. The problem here is that the principal cannot verify that the agent has behaved appropriately" (1989, 58).

The assumptions made about people in agency theory are drawn from economic theory. They are that individuals are self-interested, their rationality is *bounded*, meaning they cannot know everything in a given situation, and they seek to avoid risk (they are *risk averse*). It is also assumed that organizations are composed of principals and agents whose goals conflict (Eisenhardt 1989, 58). Self-interested employees tend to *shirk*, meaning that they try to avoid working, or will do work the employer (principal) does not want them to do. (This description of employee behavior is parallel to that of *Theory X* in the literature of organizational behavior. In Theory X, employees try to avoid working and must be supervised closely. This is contrasted with the *Theory Y* assumption of an employee who, under the appropriate type of management, is self-motivated). Principals respond to employees shirking by monitoring their behavior—for example, by creating hierarchical layers of supervision, independent teams of analysts, objective-setting and outcome measurement systems, or boards composed of people from outside the organization to observe behavior and performance.

In government, "citizens are principals, politicians are their agents. Politicians are principals, bureaucrats are their agents. Bureaucratic superiors are principals, bureaucratic subordinates are their agents. The whole of politics is therefore structured by a chain of principal–agent relationships. . . ." (Moe 1984, 765). However, the accountability of career public administrators to superiors or politicians can be relatively weak, partly because of the fact that practitioners know much more than their superiors about the conduct of their work and partly because of "slack," which is "the difference between the true minimum cost of service provision and what the bureau actually spends" (Moe 1984, 763).

Practitioners, in the public choice view of public service, want to preserve this difference in knowledge, called "information asymmetry," because it allows them to use slack to promote personal agendas. These might include incentives to subordinates, "payoffs" to allies for their support, purchase of new technology, and so on. The use of slack is one type of breakdown in accountability, of shirking; another important type is the desire of the practitioner to do something that bureaucratic or professional superiors do not want done. This often takes form as implementation of programs in a way that serves the preferences of practitioners rather than those of representatives.

The concept of agency brings into bold relief the burden of representation, a burden that falls on both those who represent citizens and the citizens themselves. Representatives must constantly seek to discover the will of a broad cross-section of community residents, and residents must constantly monitor the behavior of representatives to ensure that their interests are fairly reflected in public policy and program implementation. In the first section of this chapter I asked, "How can we recapture and maintain a sense of accountability, a linkage between citizen wishes and the actions of the governing body?" In other words, what can we do to better fulfill the accountability and democracy principles? In making changes in this direction, can we maintain the rationality principle? If so, the burden of representation may be lightened and the quality of community life improved.

The reader will note that awareness of these issues has been present in the field for decades, but the broader context of today's return to earlier values (see Chapter 1) has intensified the pressure on governing bodies. Often-conflicting citizen demands for increased scrutiny of the cost and quality of public services, fair treatment of all groups of citizens, and expanded citizen involvement have made the job of the local representative a focus of conflict and intense local debate. In this setting, it is not enough to stand by passively and hope that representatives will do the best they can. The problems, opportunities, and changes taking place in local governance make it prudent to critically examine the relationship between representatives and those they serve.

Let us accept for the moment that failures in representation can be, if not avoided altogether, then made less frequent, and that it is possible to make changes in agency-accountability relationships in local governance that simultaneously serve the democracy, accountability, and rationality principles. The next sections outline one possible path toward this goal.

Routine and Community
Interest Policy

This book is about governance and the roles of citizens, representatives, and practitioners. The central activity that brings these people together is the creation of public policy—that is, the process of determining the collective will of the community and implementing it in the form of public programs. In this chapter, I have described the problem of failure of representation and argued that governance structures should be improved to encourage self-governance and greater accountability to the public will.

It may appear reasonable to deal with the burden of representation by significantly diminishing the role of elected representation, to call for a return to the direct democracy of the town meeting or to move toward a modern version, for example, an "electronic town hall" with citizens connected by computer. Benjamin Barber's concept of "strong democracy," in which citizens engage each other in an ongoing discourse on community issues, depends on doing away with impediments like representative bodies and permitting "unmediated self-government by an engaged citizenry" (1984, 261). Barber offered a variety of unmediated processes, including neighborhood assemblies and electronic communications (already in effect in some form in many places: see Conte 1995). This move toward modern forms of direct democracy is paralleled in the public administration literature by *discourse theory,* in which the role of the representative is replaced by more direct ways of involving citizens in policy making, whether face-to-face or by other means (Fox and Miller 1995).

It seems clear that more direct citizen involvement is desirable in contemporary community governance. However, proposals to mostly do away with representative governing bodies are not particularly practical or desirable. Such proposals do not deal with the institutional history and current structures of local government, nor do they address the reality of contemporary urban management. Whether or not a community is committed to open governance and citizen discourse, the problem of ongoing, daily governance in the name of the people remains. The history of the institution of local government reveals a natural evolution from forms of direct democracy in small communities to representative democracy as size and complexity made it difficult to involve citizens in many of the functions of local government. It is one thing to advocate greater citizen self-determination, another to deal with the daily demands of running a government.

Advocates of moving from representative to citizen-driven governance largely ignore government itself, the technical–rational mechanism that performs the public services on which we depend. They ignore it in the rush to get citizens involved in talking about a reality that seems unhampered by the messy, costly, and complex process of actually doing the work of implementing policy. They are interested primarily in the "before" part of public policy—that is, the exciting part during which people define an issue and decide what to do about it. This is important, but governance is also very much about the "after" part of public policy, the part that involves carrying out pedestrian but essential tasks like monitoring implementation of budgets, making policy decisions about contracting and purchasing procedures, deciding the principles to be used in negotiations with public employee labor associations, and determining which streets to repave. Open governance and citizen discourse is important, but it cannot by itself secure sustained and coherent policy judgment and implementation week after week, year after year.

To secure that kind of rational consistency while preserving democracy and accountability, people who can lay valid claim to representing the public must be responsible for the conduct of routine policy making and implementation. These people need to be citizens, not practitioners, if community government is to be an extension of the will of the public. There not only is a role for elected officials, but if there were no elected officials, we would have to invent them just as people did long ago. There is a place in the governance process that needs to be filled by citizen representatives who perform an accountability and control function at the head of an organizational hierarchy that responds to the will of the public and directs the activities of practitioners.

The problem is how to achieve this given the burden of representation and the very real possibility of failure of representation. One way out of this apparent dilemma is to suggest a change in the role of the governing body and the role of citizens involved in policy making and implementation. Currently, it is assumed that a city, county, school, or other special district governing body is the primary decision maker about public policy and how it is carried out. They may formally delegate authority to boards or commissions in some specific functional areas (such as planning) and they may create temporary committees to study important issues. Despite the activities of these boards it remains clear to all that, in most cases, it is the governing body that both creates and oversees implementation of public policy. Representation rather than participatory citizen decision making becomes a problem when the governing body assumes sole responsibility for deciding fundamental policy, policy that is of interest to a large part of the community, as compared to routine policy matters. It is impossible to draw concrete lines between "routine" and "community interest" policy, because almost anything, in specific context, can become an issue of interest to the broader community. Most decisions that need to be made by citizens in government are routine, their importance limited to a few public service practitioners and sometimes an individual citizen or group of citizens. *Community interest* policy has broader implications for the community, involving significant change and consequences for the future.

The change, advocated in Chapter 3, from centralized governance to governance by citizen boards should relieve the governing body of lower-level routine decisions about which they lack the technical knowledge to make informed choices. However, the crucial matter is to shift much of the responsibility for the formulation (the "before" part) and implementation ("after") of community interest policy away from the governing body and toward citizen bodies. I suggest that the governing body should not be the central decision maker on community interest policy but should delegate the primary responsibility for identifying and discussing policy options to citizen boards. The governing body would retain the responsibilities of making final decisions on community interest policies and reviewing a citizen board or committee decision that may not be supportable, for example because of legal or financial concerns, violation of adopted goals or policies, or failure to follow required procedures.

This new governing body role would significantly shift policy responsibility to informed citizens rather than overburdened representatives. Thus far the change I propose in the role of the governing body has been stated only in the negative sense of limiting governing body action to final policy decisions and situations in which citizen bodies do not act appropriately. In positive terms, what sort of new role is being suggested for elected community representatives?

The Coordinating Council

We have found that elected governing bodies in local public agencies can be subject to the problem of failure of representation. Further, the potential for such failure results in a burden that falls on both representatives and citizens because representation of public will is very different from direct enactment of public will. It is one step removed from direct public will, a step that introduces a significant principal–agent problem into community governance. In the first three eras of development of the institution of community governance, the governing body was associated with elite control, democratic excess, and the support of professionalism that sometimes excluded citizen participation. This left communities open to wide and unpredictable variation in governance outcomes. For the central elected body to serve the democracy and accountability principles in the era of citizen governance, its role within the institutional structure needs to be changed.

The citizen board concept in Chapter 3 set the stage for a shift in the governing body role as citizen boards assume responsibility for policy formulation and implementation in many areas of public service delivery. Now, we add another part to the Citizen Governance model by suggesting that the governing body become, in function if not in name, the "community coordinating council." This shift in role would change the governing body's function from central decision-making body to coordinator of citizen participation, decision making, and policy and program implementation.

As coordinating council, the governing body would usually not decide policy matters of fundamental community interest by themselves. Instead, they would clarify the issues; create opportunities for a full public airing of information and concerns in ways that welcome citizens into the process and allow them to become involved on a somewhat equal footing with the politically powerful and with professional public service practitioners [see Fox and Miller's (1995) discussion of meeting the "warrants" for discourse, such that there can be sincere, relevant, and willing public discussion]; facilitate the interaction of citizens with administrative agencies; and arbitrate between competing interests, sometimes making a final decision, but by choosing between citizen-identified options, rather than deciding on their own.

The coordinating council is the people's representative not in the Burkean sense of functioning as trustees of the public interest, free to decide for the people in their absence. Instead the members of the council represent the people's interest in creating and maintaining open discourse and valid self-governance. This process of discourse would allow time to build a sense of awareness and legitimacy around public policy issues that is not provided by the pure representational role. There are examples of this within some contemporary multistage citizen involvement processes, such as the citizen involvement required in the state-mandated planning process in Oregon local government. There, it is common to have an important policy matter examined by a citizens' involvement committee, then a planning commission, then the governing body. When the matter reaches the governing body there has been time and opportunity for broad information dissemination and individual participation, so that representatives are hard-pressed to ignore citizen perceptions and desires.

In places where such multistage discourse opportunities do not exist, it is common for political acceptance to be gained in an inverted process in which the governing body meets resistance to a potential decision and either refers the matter to an existing committee or creates a special study group, thus delaying action, calming public concern, and sharing responsibility. This inverted process determines the appropriate level of decision making (the scale principle) and provides for democratic governance, accountability, and rationality in a "backwards" manner. It allows for democratic self-determination because circumstances require it rather than because it is the right thing to do.

Changing the role of the governing body from deciding matters of community interest to coordinating citizen involvement and self-determination may eventually result in modifications to local charters or state constitutions. Initially, it should be possible to move toward the new model with incremental steps supporting decentralization of specific community interest policy decisions. After a period of demonstrated success, these tentative steps can be put into standard practice by formal action. This is not a smooth or easy process, as many elected officials will be reluctant to give up a sense of control. They can be assured that the coordinating council concept does not require abandonment of ultimate policy responsibility, but instead a willingness to encourage open and honest public involvement on fundamental matters of public policy.

In a community that has fully implemented the idea of the governing body as coordinating council, much routine policy making and implementation is overseen by citizen boards in functional areas, working together with the public and public service practitioners. All matters of community interest are thoroughly and openly discussed in public settings that welcome citizens into the process of determining the future of their community. The governing body, rather than being a burden because of the possibility of failure of representation, refers matters to internal citizen bodies and outside citizen involvement groups and administrative agencies, makes final decisions in cases requiring mediation between competing interests, monitors the decision-making process for fairness and consistency, and evaluates the success of policy implementation.

Decision making in this setting is made at the "lowest" level possible (the scale principle), with plenty of opportunity for citizen involvement (the democracy principle). Elected representatives refer much policy authority to citizen bodies and are deeply involved in coordination and joint action. They ensure that citizen boards do their work with the broader public interest in mind, rather than becoming captive to interest groups or the views of practitioners with assertive agendas, thus the accountability principle is served. It is hoped that these changes in the role of the governing body and its relationship to citizens make possible more rational decision making (the rationality principle), as people take the time to study public policy issues and carefully consider the best course for their communities.

CHAPTER

Five

Practitioners

The Context of Public Service

Today's community political environment is a challenging one for the public service practitioner. As we have seen, practitioners must navigate between entrenched elites and demands for decision-making access by citizens. They must find their way between the representational failure of governing-body dominated systems and the lack of accountability and rationality in decentralized or citizen-dominated systems. They are called on, simultaneously, to offer expert advice to elected officials, exhibit deference to those same officials, provide efficient daily administration of public services with decreasing resources, and present a pleasing customer-service face to citizens. This is taking place in a nationwide macro-environment of dislike of government, tax revolt, downsizing, privatization, and bureaucrat bashing fueled by political leaders at all levels of government.

These phenomena are not surprising, given the return to values of the past discussed in Chapter 1. With movement back toward localism, small and responsive government, and the professional as adviser rather than controller of public agencies, public bureaucracies at all levels are experiencing pressure to change. The size and complexity of American government makes it difficult to generalize about the impact of these trends in a particular agency or on a specific public service practitioner.

In each local governmental unit, practitioners work within a particular community orientation toward public policy and governance, as outlined in Chapter 2: an accessible and open or excluding and closed governance system; an emphasis on marketplace or living space values; a desire for a large or restricted role for government; and acceptance of, or resistance to, professionalism. These orientations affect how practitioners approach their work and the success they have in serving their communities. Many people who have served in several local governments have observed elements of each of these orientations and, within a particular community, they have watched orientations change over time.

The complexity of the overall environment of public service, the variation in community policy orientation, and the rate of change in both the overall environment and in communities make it difficult to generalize about the nature of public service. Despite this, meaningful generalizations can be made in the contemporary setting that are helpful in sorting out how practitioners can best serve the public. These generalizations are based on the history of the practice of public service and its meaning to both practitioners and citizens. As we consider the Citizen Governance concept of the practitioner role toward the end of the chapter, it becomes apparent that the principles of community governance are well served by professional practice solidly grounded in the practices developed in the past, combined with a willingness to adapt to the future.

Evolution of the Public Service Practitioner

Early in the nation's history there were no administrative agencies to perform community services. Individuals took care of themselves and, in situations that required collective action, citizens or groups of citizens volunteered their time or were paid small stipends for their efforts. In the typical New England community, citizens were selected by their peers at the annual town meeting to perform tasks such as keeping the peace, returning wayward livestock, maintaining the roads, collecting taxes, and looking after other community needs (Cook 1976, 23–62).

Through the eighteenth century and into the nineteenth, it became common for people who took on such tasks to be paid enough to seek the work rather than to perform it only from a sense of duty. Gradually, as cities grew and volunteer or part-time workers could not handle the quantity and complexity of the work to be done, formal organizational structures emerged to provide fire, police, public health, infrastructure, schools, and other services. This history includes solving problems of technical methods, transitioning from volunteers to specialists through training and acquired experience, and dealing with occasional corruption and lack of resources. Today, we expect technical capability and efficiency from local public administrative bodies. During the twentieth century they have developed into the familiar form of well-organized bureaucratic agencies with a body of professional knowledge, expertise, and the funds to carry out their missions.

The contemporary positions held by career public service practitioners evolved from the community-minded work of early citizen volunteers. Full-time, trained dedication to public service is a model of community activity that grew slowly and with difficulty through trial and error over a period covering more than a century. The local practitioner's role evolved from that of citizen volunteer, but because of the complexity of contemporary governance and the full-time nature of the role, practitioners are now and forever different from citizens. Cooper (1984, 307) argued that "the ethical identity" of the public administrator is "that of the citizen who is employed as one of us to work for us; a kind of professional citizen ordained to do that work which we in a complex large-scale political community are unable to undertake ourselves."

This view recognizes the evolutionary connection between the citizen and the public professional. It also reflects the trend in the twentieth century (see chapter 2, p. 35) toward separating public service work from citizens, making it the province of public professionals. It relates in large part to the national level of governance, where the size of agencies and remoteness from citizen accountability often make a more direct citizen-practitioner connection impractical. At the local level, organizational size is less limiting to the role of the citizen, so that the practitioner, rather than acting instead of citizens as a surrogate, can become a facilitator of direct citizen action.

The Public Service Role

The institution of community governance is changing, from domination by the ideal of professionalized, scientific administration to the ideal of citizen self-determination. This is part of the long-term change nationwide in citizen expectations of government we have identified as returning to values of the past. The impact of this long-term change on the practitioner can be significant, though it is somewhat limited by the day-to-day reality of delivering services such as repairing the streets, investigating crimes, building parks, and so on. Except for advances in technology (such as paving machines, sophisticated crime detection equipment, and computers), the routine performance of much public work is as it always has been.

Changes in the surrounding macro-level political and economic environment mean that pressures for cost efficiency and responsiveness to citizen preferences are increasing, pushing the practitioner into new ways of approaching old tasks. Though the work is not much different, the process of deciding what to do and how to fund it is very different. It includes dialogue, deliberation, and negotiation requiring interpersonal and administrative skills seemingly unrelated to the technical tasks of service delivery.

Our contemporary understanding of the role of the public service practitioner in this setting does not spring fully formed from the events of today or the recent past, but comes from the history of community governance. This understanding includes boundaries on the *role frames* (Schon 1983, 309–14) of public service practitioners, who must carry out the basic functions of the community and receive direction, monitoring, and evaluation. Those who direct, monitor, and evaluate practitioners include interested citizens or citizen groups, economic or political leaders (*elites*), and professional peers and coworkers. This is the practitioner's *role set*, those who, over time, create "role expectations" of performance for the practitioner and give feedback when they think performance improvement or change in the role is necessary.

Our understanding of the roles of public service practitioners in communities nationwide must be broad and flexible to allow for local variation, individual choice, and vocational specialization. And it must change over time with the institution of community governance, because a view of the practitioner's role that made sense in relation to the challenges of the 1920s or 1930s can be inappropriate entering the twenty-first century.

In addition to long-term, broad change in the role of the public service practitioner, local political conditions can change rapidly, leading to variability in the community policy orientations (accessible or closed governance system, emphasis on marketplace or living space values, a large or restricted role for government, attitude toward professionalism). As policy orientations change, so do expectations of public professionals. Though there are boundaries on the range of choices practitioners can make about their roles, each practitioner can choose from among many ways to respond to the expectations of those she or he serves.

An example of the impact of local role expectations on the practitioner role can be found in the selection of city managers by city councils. Saltzstein (1974) and Flentje and Counihan (1984) found that city councils sometimes hire a relatively weak and compliant city manager after a strong one leaves for another job or is fired. In replacing a strong manager with a weak one, a council may hire a manager with a weaker commitment to professionalism or one who is not a professional city manager but an insider from the organization who is a known quantity and can be controlled more easily. Like politics at the national level, where we see fluctuations over long periods of time between conservative and liberal or Republican and Democrat administrations, local government can go through cycles of attitudes toward professionalism that have quite an effect on public administrators.

Another way to think of the role of a particular public service practitioner is to imagine a "sphere of discretion," a defined zone of possible action. Each position in a public agency occupied by a practitioner carries with it such a role sphere of discretion. Most people in the role set would find the actions within this sphere to be a logical and desirable part of the practitioner's role. The sphere of discretion rests in a larger area of possible actions that are not regarded by the role set as appropriate to this particular practitioner's role. Although the practitioner's daily activities stay within the sphere of discretion, citizens, representatives, and peers, though they may not always agree with things the practitioner does, will believe that his or her actions are those they expect of someone filling this specific role.

If the practitioner takes actions that fall outside the sphere or does less than expected within the sphere, members of the role set will become concerned and begin to question the practitioner's performance. Actions outside the sphere could include making decisions about matters usually dealt with by superiors or elected representatives, working directly with citizens in a way that makes organizational superiors or representatives feel threatened, or strongly advocating an idea or program before citizens or representatives have had an opportunity to discuss or consider it. Over time, the role sphere of discretion can change, growing larger or smaller. This can be caused by changes in the role set as members come and go, the issues and challenges facing the community change, role set responses to practitioner actions, or a practitioner request to renegotiate the contents of the role.

In an interview I conducted as part of a research project, a community planning director described his mental image of his sphere of discretion. He saw it as a "ball and chain," with the ball as the "center of political gravity," and the end of the chain attached to his ankle. For him, this was not a negative image; he was a thoughtful person who spent time mentally calculating the sphere of discretion scribed by the length of the chain. He felt he had plenty of "room to roam," or freedom to act, within his sphere and was careful about attempting to enlarge it. When he thought it necessary to take an action that might be seen as falling outside the sphere, one creating a significant change from current practice, he would discuss his ideas with role set members, discovering how receptive they might be. He preferred to have the role set incrementally incorporate such ideas into their own thinking, thus claiming ownership for the ideas and moving the focus of attention away from the planner.

The Goals of Practitioners

Relationships between practitioners and people in role sets can be influenced by a variety of personal motivations and substantive goals. Public service practitioners are motivated by a range of preferences about public policy and governance and individual motivations to act are as complex and varied as the people who work in public administration. There are substantive goals specific to areas of practice within local public administration, such as law and order in police work, improving the lives of economically disadvantaged people in social work, and so on. Despite this complexity, we can identify perspectives on the relationship of the role set and the practitioner that cut across vocational boundaries and are of broad interest to the field of public administration. Before we turn to a discussion of these perspectives, we should take into account individual practitioner calculation of the personal risks of professional action.

Personal Motivations

Practitioners are motivated to some extent by personal concerns, such as career advancement or financial security. Though these may seem like purely private, individual matters, decisions in the professional workplace are often affected by them. For example, imagine two police officers confronted with a risky and difficult choice. They have, separately, observed other officers using excessive force during on-the-street arrest situations. Both officers believe strongly that such behavior must be reported so that it does not continue, and both know that officers who report it can be subject to various kinds of retaliation from some of their peers, people who think that officers should stick together and protect each other. It could easily happen that one officer chooses to report the incident and the other chooses to be silent. In such a situation, the first officer decided that potential difficulty in the workplace could not offset the belief that reporting excessive force is the right thing to do, and the second officer decided that the consequences of displaying apparent disloyalty to peers outweighed the ethical commitment to reporting serious misbehavior.

Another relatively common example is that of the community public practitioner who believes that her or his livelihood could be threatened by speaking out on an issue. This often involves a situation in which the practitioner believes that a decision should be based on rational, professional knowledge of an issue, or it should be the result of a process that involves the community, whereas influential people would rather decide it on the basis of potential impact on their interests and without public input. The practitioner faces the choice of acting on norms of professional conduct or acting out of a desire to preserve personal career status and economic security. It may seem clear that the right choice is the professionally correct one, but practitioners can only be expected to assume a certain level of risk and uncertainty in their personal lives as a result of their commitment to public service.

Many times, the personal motivations of practitioners agree with the demands of organizations. When they do not, practitioners must calculate the balance between the risk and the value of the goals to be achieved. Practitioners may not be aware of this calculation in some situations. But in others, they are very much aware of the stress and difficulty of deciding whether to be safe or take the risky actions they believe to be right.

Value-Free Neutrality

Turning from personal motivations for action to substantive professional concerns, a good way to begin is with the substantive goal that is the least assertive or outwardly apparent to the role set. Many public professionals view themselves as neutral, highly proficient implementers of policy determined by others. Neutral professionals are presumably "value-free," because they do not decide what should be done, only how to do it. The idea of neutrality comes from the reform impulse of the late nineteenth and early twentieth centuries and the challenges of administering the emerging urban–industrial society of that time.

Despite the declared lack of values in the idea of neutrality, supposedly neutral practitioners often espouse the paired values of economy and efficiency, which are long-accepted measures of successful community governance (Stillman 1974, 20–2). Especially in this time of scarce resources and public scrutiny of government services, economy and efficiency are important practitioner goals. Privatization, reinventing, reengineering, and similar trends in the field are evidence of the pervasiveness of these goals and, although they can help produce better public services at reduced cost, they can also replace other goals and have impacts on the democracy and accountability principles if practitioners strive to fulfill them at the cost of including citizens in decision making.

In public administration we often use an essay written in 1887 by Woodrow Wilson, then a college professor, as an indicator of the concerns of the field at the beginning of what would become modern public administration. Wilson urged adoption of "scientific" methods of public management and greater separation between the process of determining policy and the process of carrying it out. As Dwight Waldo (1981, 65) has noted, the "politics–administration" relationship is the focus of much thinking and writing in public administration, as well as being a major part of the daily work life of many public practitioners, and any study of the role of the public administrator must take it into account.

We know today that the neutral professional model cannot fully explain the reality of public service. This is because many, if not most, practitioners are involved in helping to shape public policy as well as implement it. Even so, the idea of neutrality fits well with an image of democratic governance by the people rather than by career professionals, an image that is deeply embedded in American political culture. For this reason, it remains a powerful way to describe the idea that public professionals are different from citizens or representatives, even when professionals are as much a part of the process of creating policy as are citizens and representatives.

In the last half of the twentieth century, the "public choice" perspective on the role of the professional became well known. It advocates policy neutrality for the practitioner, but with greater emphasis on control of the bureaucracy. In the public choice view, public professionals are "agents" to the representatives and citizens who determine policy and should not themselves take part in the policy process. The term "public choice" does not mean choices made by citizens deliberating together over public policy issues. Instead, following basic economic assumptions that focus on individual preferences and self-interest, it means that individual citizen choices about policy or political candidates are aggregated (through voting) to determine the majority will.

Public choice theorists view the public sector as simply another kind of market; the medium of exchange in the private sector is money and in the public sector it is votes (Downs 1957). Though many of us think of the motivations of people in public service as being different from those of people in the private sector, the public choice theorist sees little difference. Thus, "if the individual is motivated by personal benefits and costs when making decisions as a consumer, worker, or investor, that individual is going to be motivated by personal benefits and costs when making decisions in the voting booth, in the halls of Congress, and in the conference rooms of the bureaucracy" (Johnson 1991, 13).

The public choice view of career public service practitioners is not flattering. Public choice theorists tend to see them as "budget maximizers" out to increase the size of their agencies so they can have larger salaries, bigger offices, more benefits, and other things of value to them personally (Niskanen 1971; 1991). To avoid this problem, the ideal public employee should function as a delegate of the elected representatives of the people. This view of the practitioner role fits with the antigovernment attitudes of the 1980s and 1990s. It can be seen in the movement toward smaller and more efficient government, for example through privatization and applying private-sector management techniques to government, such as Total Quality Management, the customer service orientation, pay-for-performance, "reinventing" and "reengineering."

Management fads are not new in public administration; the public sector often imports ideas from the private sector for a time, then either discards them or incorporates parts of them in modified form to suit the unique circumstances of public organizations. This can be said of program-planning-budgeting (PPB), management-by-objectives (MBO), zero-base budgeting (ZBB), and quality circles. However, economic and private-sector concepts of organizational purpose and management have had a significant impact on public administration in the last two decades of the twentieth century and, given the general climate of public attitude toward government, they may be expected to influence public practice into the twenty-first century.

Paradoxically, the use of economic concepts in the public sector has also produced a demand for public practitioners to break out of their bureaucratic confines, managing the public's business like private sector businesses, behaving like "entrepreneurs" rather than tightly controlled agents. These public entrepreneurs are expected to act like business executives, finding ways for their organizations to get "a piece of the action" (Osborne and Gaebler 1993, 200) by becoming involved in public–private partnerships and speculation in shopping centers, golf courses, hotels, convention centers, and similar typically private-sector ventures. The public agency's ability to restrict and direct the use of land, create special taxing districts for improvements, and sell bonds to generate development capital allows it to intervene in the market, creating surplus resources that can be invested in community amenities or new enterprises.

For public professionals to mimic the behavior of their private-sector counterparts, they must adopt some of their characteristics, such as "autonomy, a personal vision of the future, secrecy, and risk-taking" (Terry 1993, 393). This is not what Americans traditionally expect from public professionals or from public agencies. The impulse to blend the public and private sectors, to "run government like a business," ignores the gulf of values and purposes that separates the two sectors. There is no question that good public managers look for ways to improve the delivery of public services, and always have. But carried too far, running government like a business can be a threat to the democracy and accountability principles as agencies and practitioners take action on their own to maximize efficiency and financial return rather than involving citizens in shaping communities that serve the citizens' values and purposes. Ultimately, the question is whether community residents are consumers of an efficiently delivered product or citizens collectively deciding the fate of their communities.

There is a danger associated with the traditional reform-era model of neutrality and a separation of policy making and administration. This danger is the tendency of practitioners to resist the value shifts described in this book as returning to values of the past by keeping elected representatives and citizens as far away from their work as possible. Highly skilled practitioners may come to regard their work as beyond the understanding of citizens who, if they ask questions or request a meaningful share in the decision-making process about public programs, are viewed as a nuisance and waste of time. Practitioners who resist citizen claims to govern programs in their communities often think of citizen self-governance as a violation of the principle of separation of politics and administration.

Resistance to perceived intrusion or micromanagement by nonprofessionals into administrative affairs is not uncommon in government, though it becomes harder to sustain in the contemporary environment of a return to earlier, citizen-driven values of governance. Though we need to recognize that citizen involvement in administration must be moderated through use of professional methods and respect for due process of law, pushing citizens and their representatives away from the conduct of their government violates the democracy and accountability principles.

Legitimacy

One way to counter the "downslope of the wave of reform" trend of skepticism about government and resulting efforts toward downsizing and control is to elevate the status of public administration. In this view, public professionals, instead of the agents of elected representatives and citizens, become a "legitimate" part of government with approximately equal standing in the formation and implementation of public policy alongside legislators and citizens. Legitimacy would mean giving greater autonomy in public governance to public service practitioners, and it has become an important model in the literature of public administration.

Those desiring increased legitimacy as a goal for public administration often focus on the national level of government. The question of legitimacy centers on the relationship of public administration to the Constitution and the nature of the founding period (Rohr 1986, 1993; Spicer and Terry 1993; Stivers 1993; Wamsley et al. 1987). Though there is confusion about what is meant by legitimacy (Warren 1993, 250–2), a legitimized public administration would seem to be one that is respected by the public, has more control, authority, and discretion to act independently than at present, and is given the status of a somewhat equal partner in relation to elected leaders and other parts of government.

Legitimacy may seem to be a good idea because the complexity of modern society causes political leadership to be ineffectual and because citizens have lost the capacity to carry out their citizenship responsibilities as a result of ignorance or indifference. If this is true, the expertise of public professionals can be used to steer government out of its morass. Carried to its logical extreme, the search for legitimacy might culminate in a guardian class of administrators who make decisions that they believe citizens choose not to make or cannot make competently (Fox and Cochran 1990).

Because of fundamental American political values, the impact of the legitimacy model of the practitioner's role seems to have been minimal. Asking for greater practitioner status in the policy-making process may soothe people irritated with what they perceive as the unfortunate effects of bureaucrat bashing or conservative ideology. The problem with the idea of greater "legitimacy" for public professionals is that most Americans simply will not accept it. It is not necessary to characterize the time in which we live as one of great skepticism about government to reach this conclusion. At any time, Americans, faced with the idea of a powerful and independent administrative class, would ask questions such as, "What would change if we had it?" "Why should we expect these people to do any 'better' than our politicians, or for that matter the bureaucrats of totalitarian states?" and "Why should I give away whatever ability I have to decide the fate of my community to a clique of non-accountable technicians?"

The idea of legitimacy runs into the same difficulties as practitioner resistance to citizen self-governance. It is in opposition to the three values of the past and could violate the democracy and accountability principles. If the purpose of local public administration is to help people create the communities they want, demanding equal status with those who legitimately "own" communities may accomplish little more than generating citizen opposition. Public service practitioners need to be experts ready to assist citizens in fulfilling their vision of the future but, as Charles Goodsell noted,

> Our craft knowledge must not become a source of technological arrogance, according to which only we know. Our official responsibilities and authority must never develop into an egotism that refuses to accept opposition or criticism. . . . We must always regard part of our job to consist of engaging in open and authentic dialogue with as many people as possible who are affected by our work. (1996, 49)

Development Versus Sustainability

There is increasing pressure on many public professionals to be skilled in "economic development," an area of practice that involves techniques for making the community attractive to new or expanding business. The goal of economic development is linked conceptually to the growth machine phenomenon discussed in Chapter 2, in which elites who benefit from land speculation and development push their communities to compete with one another for economic advantage. It can be good for professional careers for practitioners to orient their relationship to the role set around the substantive goal of economic development. By doing so, they help the economic elite and can become highly "marketable," eligible for promotion or advancement to better jobs in other places. In the past decade or so, a trend toward emphasis on economic development has been evident in the advertisements for certain public management specialties, such as planning and community development and city management.

The substantive goal of environmental protection or community sustainability can be directly opposed to the goal of economic development. The practitioner who chooses to act based on the idea of "fostering quality of person, community, and environment" (Nelson and Weschler 1996, 13) simultaneously takes on a task that runs counter to much of the political essence of American communities. The linkage between community policy making and the powerful people who benefit from physical and economic growth is a strong one. There are many community practitioners who contribute to this goal through their work in areas such as parks, social services, and economic improvement that involves strengthening local businesses that employ local people. However, it is not often that practitioners have the opportunity to assess the community as an integrated system that, if managed properly, can serve the needs of people while using land and resources in a way that preserves their productive capacity and aesthetic beauty for future generations.

Social Equity

Attention given by public administration academicians and practitioners to the goal of social equity grew out of a belief in the 1960s that America had become dangerously divided by class and economic status. The counter-cultural revolution, racial uprisings in American cities, and resistance to the Vietnam War served as evidence for some that social institutions and leaders were preserving gross inequities in wealth and opportunities for self-determination that had to be changed by radical action.

Some public administration academicians responded to these conditions with proposals to change the relationship of public professionals to their political superiors and society at large. According to Dwight Waldo, these proposals included *client-centered* or *street-level* services to reduce bureaucratic obstacles for citizens, participation of client populations in governing public programs, and creating a public bureaucracy that was *representative,* in the sense that public professionals would be similar to the citizenry in relation to geography, class, race, and other factors (1981, 95–6).

These ideas came to be known as the *New Public Administration.* To the extent that one believes that existing political structures and leaders favor the wealthy and powerful at the expense of the weak and powerless, the New Public Administration shift of decision-making focus from elected representatives to street-level bureaucrats and their clients is logical. It also can be threatening to those elected representatives and to those who view them as the rightful and legal locus of the power of the people to govern themselves. In his book *Without Sympathy or Enthusiasm,* Victor Thompson found the premises of New Public Administration to be "a most amazing effort to establish a new claimant [to public power] in place of the owner (that is, in place of the public). It is a brazen attempt to 'steal' the popular sovereignty" (1975, 66).

Facilitating Citizen Discourse

For practitioners who do not wish to advocate a particular policy outcome but believe in the democracy principle, an appropriate goal is to encourage open public discourse and decision making (this goal is the basis for the "helper" role, discussed in the section that follows). Pursuing this goal is not passive or risk free, because it carries with it the dual risks of retaliatory action by the elite or citizen-chosen policy outcomes with which the practitioner may strongly disagree. Action toward fulfilling the goal of citizen self-determination may rest on the conceptual foundation of critical theory, as described in Chapter 3. This foundation includes enlightening citizens, giving them knowledge and the opportunity to use it. This leads to "emancipation," as citizens have the tools needed to make a difference in the future of their communities.

The reader may think of other practitioner goals common across the field of public administration. For the purposes of this book, the goals we have discussed provide a good foundation for thinking about types of roles practitioners adopt in their daily work.

Three Practitioner Role Types

Earlier in this chapter we discussed concepts related to the role of the public service practitioner, including the role set, role expectations, and the sphere of discretion. Now, we can create a typology of roles that incorporates these concepts and makes it easier for us to apply them to specific situations. The literature of public administration contains many role typologies for public practitioners, organized around a variety of issues, such as practitioner motivations, how they interact with citizens, the practitioner's legal or constitutional obligations, how they organize agencies and supervise their employees, and so on. In this book, we are especially concerned with the relationship of practitioners to citizens and elected representatives and the way they become involved in the creation and implementation of public policy. (For an excellent overview of public administration roles, see Kass and Catron 1990.)

Practitioner involvement in public policy is the subject of the typology offered here, which describes three practitioner roles. One of these is the *implementer* role: Implementers are "neutral" practitioners who avoid significant involvement in shaping policy. Another, the *controller* role, includes practitioners who seek to influence the outcomes of the policy process. Implementers and controllers are located at polar ends of a continuum we could label *practitioner intent to influence public policy*. Between the polar ends of this continuum may be found an infinite number of intermediate positions, but for our purposes we will identify just one, the *helper* role. Helpers take an active part in policy creation and implementation by serving to interpret public wishes for representatives, presenting professional knowledge of organizational and technical practices to citizens and representatives, and monitoring decision making and implementation to ensure that citizens have opportunities to participate.

The apparent goals of implementers are to dutifully carry out lawful policy directions in a professional and competent manner and to avoid the potential trouble and risk associated with direct involvement in determining public policy. They may have strong feelings about the substantive issues dealt with in the previous section, but they keep such thoughts to themselves. Where professional service values of efficiency or effectiveness are at stake, implementers will take care that appropriate people hear of their concerns, but they avoid going outside accepted formal channels of communication. Many people who serve in public agencies are implementers or have observed implementers. Often, implementers are valued colleagues, providing competent service without causing disturbance or pushing for change. Sometimes, when they serve in positions that require leadership or innovation, their lack of initiative and assertiveness can hamper agency effectiveness.

Controllers seek to guide the policy process and outcomes by influencing the attitudes of their superiors or of elected officials or citizens. Though we know it is unrealistic to expect a clear separation between policy making and administration, controllers sometimes push the boundaries of accepted professional practice by going outside the normal hierarchy, interacting directly with high-level organizational officials, elected representatives, or citizens to mobilize opinion in favor of a particular policy or to influence the outcome of a policy creation process already under way. They are "true believers" crusading for their vision of how the community should be organized and what the end result of public action should be. It is with the controller role that the substantive goals discussed previously become especially apparent and important.

The behavior of controllers can be risky for themselves and for the community. It is important for those of us in public administration to understand this role behavior because it occurs at the boundaries of what is commonly accepted as appropriate for public practitioners in a democratic society. Controller behavior can be an exciting and worthwhile source of new ideas and policy innovation, but it can also be a threat to control of public governance by citizens and their representatives, placing the professional in a situation much like that of the elected official, leading the way in shaping public opinion to conform with the controller's vision of the community future.

Practitioners who act as "helpers" often are interested in certain public policy outcomes in the community, but their focus is on the process of dialogue and deliberation that leads to policy decisions and program implementation. Like controllers, helpers may go outside the formal hierarchy, but they do so to reach the goal of citizen self-governance, allowing citizens to select the substantive results they prefer. The section that follows devotes more attention to the helper role, as it is the one advocated in the Citizen Governance model.

Of course, the implementer, helper, and controller are "pure" types, drawn to illustrate a range of intent to shape policy; a given individual may exhibit mixtures of the role types and may change from one role type to another in different situations. There is another important dimension of practitioner behavior in relation to citizens that cuts across the implementer-helper-controller policy to influence typology. This is the practitioner's desire to limit access to the everyday machinery of administration by citizens or elected representatives. We are just as likely to see an implementer try to limit citizen access to the tasks and processes of administration as we are a controller, and a helper may do this as well. The rationale for keeping "outsiders" away from the details of administration (aspects of personnel actions, budgeting, and specific decisions about programs) is that they are not professionals, cannot understand the technical realities of program administration, and would only cause confusion, delay, and irrationality if they "intrude" into expert administration.

There are two very important problems with excluding citizens and representatives from administration. These problems were identified in Chapter 3 in the discussion of the individual knowledge limit. The first is that, without knowledge of administration, citizens and representatives cannot make informed decisions about the creation and implementation of policy; this violates the rationality principle.

Second, if the public or its representatives are not informed about how the affairs of the members of the community are being administered, there is potential for abuse of administrative discretion. However well-intentioned public professionals may be, distance from the watchful eye of the "owners" of the community can lead to actions that strike the ordinary citizen as odd, inappropriate, biased in favor of particular groups or people, or simply incompetent. The actions that come to light, possibly on the pages of the local newspaper, often seem trivial in themselves. Recent examples from the author's community include paying for managers to have four-wheel drive-vehicles for personal use, paying a former mayor a large sum for the privilege of building a water line across his property, and giving unusually large salary bonuses to senior staff at a public hospital. Even if relatively minor on their face, situations like these can convey an impression of abuse, arrogance, and insensitivity to the values and expectations of the tax-paying public.

In addition to these minor actions that can be irritating to public opinion, on occasion actions may be taken away from public view that have serious, possibly far-reaching implications. These could include decisions about how to plan for growth, such as whether the public or developers should pay the costs of new infrastructure, or decisions about whether to reallocate resources (street improvements, policing, education and daycare assistance for single parents, and so on) into troubled neighborhoods, or crucial safety-related decisions such as where to locate fire stations and how to staff them. Excluding the public from important,

community-interest policy issues breaks the chain of accountability, violating the accountability principle.

Of course, it is possible for citizens or representatives to
become so involved in the details of administration that they
really do impede effective action; the rationality principle can be
violated if administration becomes deprofessionalized, just as it
can if citizen or representative decision making is based on insufficient information. This is a matter of balance, of finding an
understanding about the practitioner role that fulfills the rationality and accountability principles in a given community at a
specific point in time.

The Helper and the Paradox of "Giving Away"

With others in public administration, I have argued that it no
longer makes sense for the goals of neutrality or legitimacy to be
primary guides to public service roles. (Adams et al., 1990; Box
1995a, 1995b; Fox and Miller 1995). This is because the social and
political context of the three values of the past puts practitioners
in a situation in which

> One, professionals can survive by opting out of the policy
> dialogue and playing safe. Two, professionals can resist the
> current cycle of change, clinging to the traditional control-
> oriented model as long as possible as events pass them by.
> Three, professionals can enter into the stream of change and
> dialogue, by their participation tempering outcomes with pro-
> fessional rationality. (Box 1995b, 89)

When we discuss role options for practitioners, we need to
be careful how we use the concepts of time and change. Preferred
practitioner roles will change in the long term. They are changing
now, as we move from an era of reform, institution building, and
technical expertise, into an era of citizen self-governance. This
movement is accompanied by pressures for change in the role of

the public service practitioner. Change is always with us and roles will change with the times.

In the short term, individual practitioners have always been able to choose role positions based on circumstances. The implementer, helper, or controller roles each can be appropriate at different times during interactions with the public, elected officials, or peers, and in varying circumstances. As a practitioner works on a project or handles a series of events, he or she thinks about desired outcomes for the current situation and considers the ways members of the role set will react to various action choices. These thoughts shape the practitioner's role choices.

Because of long-term role change and the reality of short-term flexibility, we need to accept the importance of all possible role choices to public service. However, the theme of the Citizen Governance model is change, understanding and adapting to societal trends and needs within the framework of the history and characteristics of the institution of community governance. I believe that as we move fully into the twenty-first century and the era of Citizen Governance, the implementer and controller roles will continue as useful alternatives for public service practitioners. I also believe that the helper role will become the most important in our thinking about how practitioners serve their communities.

If we deemphasize the quest for professional neutrality or greater legitimacy, the task is to build better relationships between public service practitioners and citizens and representatives. The issue is how to combine the practitioner's unavoidably subservient position in the hierarchy of public organizations with a proactive stance in relation to public policy formulation and implementation. The position of the public service practitioner is unavoidably subservient because practitioners are employees, agents of the public through their elected representatives, and these elected representatives have the power to remove and replace practitioners. Rather than protest this position or try to wall ourselves off from the world with claims of a policy–administration separation, we need to seek constructive ways to be a part of the exciting institutional changes underway.

The logic of my argument for the helper role as a central feature of Citizen Governance is, on a superficial level, that of process of elimination: The implementer and controller roles are inadequate in the contemporary situation, so the helper role is what remains, in the middle of the continuum of intent to affect policy creation and implementation. But the helper role of the public service practitioner is not only what remains after other possibilities are eliminated. Rather, it is a role model built on a foundation of critical theory and the history of the institution of community governance, a history of citizens striving for a balance of administrative rationality and citizen self-determination.

The Citizen Governance model explicitly recognizes the political constraints inherent in the ecology of public administration practice. We recognize that the community practitioner is usually employed directly or indirectly by people who wield political power because of their control of the private market. Though the partially democratic nature of our political system allows some public access to the policy process, the reality of elite control based on power and wealth cannot be avoided. Because members of the public are often not aware of this control of the policy process, they cannot effectively participate in public governance nor step outside their situation to evaluate the need for change.

In contrast to the controller role in which practitioners become the focus of meaningful change, advocating for substantive goals such as social equity, the helper aims to create conditions in which a fully conscious public enacts change. This involves pursuing the critical theory goals of enlightening citizens and giving them access to the policy dialogue, thereby empowering, or "emancipating," them to act. In this way, helpers function as "facilitators, educators, and coparticipants, rather than deference-demanding experts or independently responsible decision makers" (Adams et al. 1990, 235–6). They "learn humility and respect for the developmental potential of others and to enjoy apparently self-limiting transfers of authority and responsibility to citizens" (Adams et al. 1990, 236).

Helpers do not strive for greater power, autonomy, and recognition. Instead, they give away knowledge and thus the power to make decisions to the people who are affected by those decisions. Paradoxically, this giving away of control makes practitioners more rather than less effective, as community residents, informed by practitioners, understand the issues and insist on meaningful change. The knowledge the helper gives away is knowledge of the practice of community governance that has been gathered over decades, centuries, by all the people who have worked to build a better future for their communities. It is a rich legacy to pass on to those who join today in the stream of people experimenting with new ideas in the process of changing the institution of community governance.

Giving away control and knowledge can be a hard thing to do. Many practitioners have been trained to maintain a separation between themselves and the public, because they are the experts and citizens are the "customers," people who know little about public services except the end products they receive and the fees or taxes they pay. Such practitioners use "mystery and mastery" of knowledge (Schon 1983, 229) to maintain separation between themselves and their clients and it can be frightening to think of letting go of this control.

There also can be significant risks to the helper role. These risks can be of two types. One is that helpers may be disciplined or fired for stirring up political currents disliked by representatives or by powerful citizens. The other is that the public may not do what practitioners think it ought to do. Once citizens are given the information needed to take part in policy dialogue and the access to the process needed to take meaningful action, they may make choices that directly contradict the substantive goals held by the public professionals who enabled them to make those choices. For example, citizens may take a stand against construction of public housing when involved practitioners may be concerned about social equity. Another example would be a citizen-driven policy process that results in development decisions that could harm the environment, whereas the practitioners who helped citizens study the options and make choices are committed to the substantive goal of environmental protection and sustainability. This latter risk is one the helper must be prepared to take, because emancipation means empowerment to act, to allow people to make their own choices when fully informed of the alternatives available to them. In so doing, as Cooper put it, the public practitioner "is responsible for upholding the sovereignty of the people while also making available to them certain technical skills and knowledge" (1991, 167).

The helper's role posture of assisting in the development of a meaningful citizen dialogue (for those citizens who wish to become involved) can be especially risky in situations in which the motives and interests of economic and political elites are substantially different from those of citizens generally. Citizens may not realize that such a difference exists, thus there is relative peace in the community; but if public practitioners supply them with the knowledge needed to understand their situation and enter the policy dialogue, elites may come to regard both citizens and practitioners as a threat to the established order (Box 1995a). In so doing, public service practitioners become an active part of the substance as well as the process of governance, communicating to citizens the essence of the institution including its practices and available policy options, helping them arrive through discourse at outcomes that are acceptable to the majority and respectful of the minority.

The evolving Citizen Governance practitioner role described in this book carries with it the burden of special knowledge and the responsibility to serve not only a person, a group, or the practitioner's personal preferences or opinion based on experience, but rather the goal of offering the opportunity for open community discourse on matters of collective importance. Recognizing that every discourse opportunity is bounded by the specific organizational-political-legal setting in which it rests and that coercion by the powerful is always a possibility, this evolving role allows the best chance at free and open discourse in search of fulfilling the democracy and rationality principles.

Six

Citizen Governance

The Principles of Community Governance

At the end of Chapter 1, I wrote that the ideas presented in this book are intended to answer the questions, "What will be the challenges of community governance?" and "What should be done to meet these challenges?" The answer given in this chapter is a three-pronged approach to citizenship, elected service, and professional practice called Citizen Governance. This approach is designed as a pragmatic response to the social and political reality of the times, expressed in the "three values of the past": localism, small and responsive government, and the professional as adviser, not controller.

Although I have offered specific suggestions in Chapters 3, 4, and 5 for the practice of governing communities, I do not mean to suggest that good governance comes only from following these ideas. On the contrary, citizens in each community need to chart their own courses, selecting practices that best accomplish their goals. Boynton and Wright said that

> both students and practitioners of urban governance should cease to be doctrinaire about specific governmental forms and should concentrate instead upon the development of mecha-

nisms which will allow for the development of the functional prerequisites of governmental leadership in the urban community regardless of the name given to the form. (1971, 35)

The thrust of this book is my argument that the way to find the practices best suited to the community is to use the principles of community governance (scale, democracy, accountability, rationality) as a primary guide. To concentrate on specific solutions instead of the principles we want to achieve is to lose sight of the forest and become lost in the trees. We have identified the challenges of community governance in the three values of the past and the community policy orientations. They are the challenges of meeting increasing citizen desire for self-governance in a political context that often makes it hard to achieve.

For citizens, elected representatives, and public service practitioners to be successful in this setting requires a clear vision of the ideas and values that are most important, of the kind of community they want in the future. The principles of community governance are drawn from the history and practice of American local governance. They do not in themselves contain a preference for a particular substantive goal, but instead help us to make value-based choices about goals. Though they are broad in scope, they are powerful tools to shape daily action when applied with persistence, courage, flexibility, and creativity. The community shaped by these principles can be envisioned by the content of the principles themselves. Such a community is a place where: action is taken at the "lowest" level consistent with good decision making; free and open discourse and decision making are practiced; there is a direct linkage in accountability from citizens to the creation and implementation of public programs; and public decision making is recognized as an important enterprise that deserves careful deliberation.

Application of the principles is not easy. To say that it requires persistence means that long-term goals are often lost in the daily problem-solving environment. To say that it requires flexibility and creativity means that there is no one best solution and that people must expect, understand, and work with a variety of different viewpoints.

To say that successful application of the principles requires courage is perhaps the most important. As we have seen in earlier parts of this book, the concepts advocated have been contested throughout our history and probably will always be objects of intense feeling and disagreement. For everyone involved in community governance, citizens, representatives, and practitioners, advocacy of the principles of community governance carries risk, ranging from frustration and disillusionment to consequences involving loss of position in the community. Deciding whether to pursue the principles means deciding how much they matter in a world in need of the values they express. As Stephen K. Bailey wrote, "perhaps the most essential courage in the public service is the courage to decide" (1964, 242). Such courage stems from "ambition, a sense of duty, and a recognition that inaction may be quite as painful as action" (241). Inaction in public organizations often results from exercise of caution or from the large and cumbersome nature of bureaucracy. However, "buck-passing which stems from lack of moral courage is the enemy of efficient and responsible government. The inner satisfactions which come from the courage to decide are substantial; but so are the slings and arrows which are invariably let loose by those who are aggrieved by each separate decision" (242).

In this concluding chapter, let us review and pursue further our discussions in the preceding chapters of the significant features of the Citizen Governance model. I will end by outlining some practical steps people can take toward implementing the model.

The Community Context

Understanding the political, social, and economic surroundings of the local public agency is essential to success in governance. Citizens, representatives, and practitioners know that they work in a complex and changing local environment that strongly influences policy development and implementation. In Chapter 2 we examined several aspects of this environment. In this concluding chapter, I want to highlight important ideas from that discussion that are especially useful to people involved in the daily work of community affairs. These ideas build toward a summation of the political context of communities in the community policy orientations.

First, we have identified **eras in the development of the institution of community governance,** stretching from the pre-Revolutionary period to the present: elite control, democracy, professionalism, and citizen governance. This is a rich and exciting history of people searching for ways to improve community life in a growing country while preserving the values of liberty and individual responsibility. In the earliest era, community governance was largely the province of economically better-off citizens with the time to devote to it. As local government delivered more services, many citizens volunteered their time to carry out functions such as policing, taking care of those in need, maintaining roads, and so on.

In the nineteenth century, government became more complex and open to democratic citizen access. Perceived inefficiency and corruption associated with machine politics and citizen boards led to professionalism in the twentieth century. With the growth of modern bureaucracies and separation of citizens from the daily tasks of governing, we are experiencing a reaction to bureaucracy and professionalism (the "downslope of the wave of reform") in public opinion. This is evident in the desire of many citizens to return to values of the past, such as localism, small and responsive government, and the professional as adviser, not controller, of public agencies.

Second, part of the legacy of the history of American community governance is interest in the questions of the **scope and structure of government.** The scope of government has always been a question in the United States; from the beginning, people wondered whether a minimal government (Jefferson's view) or a larger and energetic government (Hamilton's view) would be best. The intensity of feeling among Americans about this issue continues, and it is the subject of public debate at every level of government. Presidential and congressional politics deal with the scope of government, as do state and local politics. People talk about downsizing, devolution, and privatization on one side, and they worry about the impacts on service delivery and individual lives on the other.

At the time the Constitution was created, a primary question was how to structure the government to allow for effective governance while preserving individual liberties. The Constitutional Founders crafted a structure of balanced powers intended to minimize opportunities for one branch of government or any person or interest group to become dominant. At the local level, people have experimented with structures throughout the nation's history, doing so on the assumption that structure is an effective way to carry their values into practice. In short, people believe that structure matters. In today's era of citizen governance, the thrust is toward structures that allow for citizen access to public policy making and implementation. This thrust is away from bureaucratic, hierarchical, and centralized structures created during the twentieth century effort to professionalize public service.

Third, in small New England communities of the past, major public decisions were made by most of the citizens who were eligible to participate in town affairs. They gathered together in the annual town meeting, discussed and decided on matters of importance, and selected from among their members those who would carry out town functions during the next year. But in the larger, modern community, this communal sort of decision making is impractical. Even if it was possible to get a large percentage of citizens into a single meeting place, only a few people would come, they would not be very representative of the whole citizen body, and important public decisions must be made throughout the year, not only at one time.

For these reasons, we have developed governance structures built around a relatively small governing body elected by the people to make decisions for us. This is an efficient way to make decisions for the public, but much can be lost. Today, governing bodies are increasingly removed from public opinion, because citizens have become accustomed to letting someone else do the work of governing for them, and because a small group of elected representatives cannot be knowledgeable about the full range of community service functions and daily activities.

In this situation it is likely that public service practitioners have to fill in for the lack of direction from citizens and representatives, making decisions that, over time, are the equivalent of significant policy positions; such decisions may not be the ones citizens would make if fully informed and given the opportunity for self-determination. To the extent that representatives shape policy, they may do so lacking the knowledge necessary for informed choice, and they may represent the views and interests of a select few rather than the community as a whole. This is the problem of **failure of representation,** in which **loop democracy** separates citizens from the policy making and implementation process by the intervening structure of representation.

Thus, communities bear a **burden of representation** because the structure of representation imposes a cost borne by most citizens. This cost consists of the degree to which public policies do not reflect the will of an informed population. In places in which disagreements among community members about representation become so intense that there is evidence of failure of representation, such as occasional recall elections, the burden of representation is a serious problem. In many other places, it may be measured only in the degree to which the community would be a different place to live if citizens had full access and opportunity to participate in governance.

Fourth, it is natural that individuals and groups seek to gain **control of the policy process** to further their interests. Where government provides just a few basic services at minimal levels, this desire to exert control causes relatively little problem. But if government grows to the point that it provides a variety of services and reaches into many areas of people's private lives, then it offers many opportunities for control.

In Chapter 2, we examined the debate about who should control public decision making in communities. It makes sense that people who have a large financial stake in a place should have an influential voice in determining public policy. So, predictably, business and property owners are well represented in the ranks of those who serve on governing bodies and are in other ways prominent in setting the course of the community. The realm of decision-making options at the local level is limited because the state and national levels of government assume responsibility for many public policies and programs. The use of physical assets such as land, buildings, and infrastructure is the primary sphere of economic and political activity in which local people have significant control, and for this reason it tends to be the focus of local politics.

The problem for our model of Citizen Governance is that often the desire of influential people to have a voice in community affairs becomes control of the public policy agenda to the extent that the average citizen is excluded from participating meaningfully. This means that citizens may feel shut out entirely or, if allowed to participate, they may find that such participation is "token," that they are not allowed to effectively influence public action. This violates the democracy principle and creates a one-sided process.

Community Policy Orientations

This review of the eras of community governance, the scope and structure of government, the burden of representation, and control of the policy process leads us to ask how these features of the public life of communities affect the daily tasks of decision making and administration. The answer within the Citizen Governance model is expressed in the community policy orientations: an accessible and open or closed and excluding governance system, an emphasis on the community as marketplace (exchange value) or as living environment (use value), a desire for a large or restricted role for government, and acceptance of, or resistance to, professionalism.

These are four pairs of opposing values that help us understand the range of action options available to citizens, representatives, and practitioners. They do not remain constant nor are the pairs mutually exclusive. Thus, community policy orientations change over time as issues develop and are resolved, as people move in and out of the policy dialogue, and as economic and demographic conditions change. And, in a given community, an observer might find unexpected combinations of policy orientations, for example an open governance system along with an emphasis on community as marketplace, desire for a restricted governmental role, and acceptance of professionalism.

Also, these orientations are the reflection of values that tend to be dominant in policy processes and outcomes. This does not mean that the whole community is in agreement with these dominant values or orientations. Often, there is a vigorous debate and disagreement over community orientations, and there are often splits between political factions or between political and economic leaders and the broader population. The balance of power in these relationships depends on which groups of people devote the time and effort necessary to control the outcome of the policy dialogue.

The many potential combinations of policy orientations can have tremendous impact on individual lives and the future of a community. A closed governance system means that citizens who want to take part in determining the future may be prevented from doing so. An orientation by political and economic leaders toward community as marketplace may conflict with the desires of a majority of residents, who are more interested in the aesthetics of the living environment. If the leaders prevail, many people will feel deprived of the community they prefer.

Practitioners working in a closed governance system must be wary of appearing to favor citizen involvement over the wishes of the leaders. They must adapt their actions to the closed setting, just as they must adapt to an orientation toward the marketplace or living environment orientations. This is not to say that they cannot work to change these orientations, only that they must tailor their behaviors to local conditions if they want to stay in the organization.

Practitioners can be profoundly influenced by the politics of orientations about the role of government and its professionals. Working in a place in which the public sector is thought of as an important part of local life is very different from working in a community where government is expected to be limited and inconspicuous. And working in a place that favors rational, technical, professional administration is very different from working in a place that favors practitioners who are seen and not heard, who take little or no part in the public policy dialogue and wait to be told what to do.

The degree to which people, whether citizens, representatives, or practitioners, are affected by community policy orientations depends on their personal values and their tolerance for divergence between personal views and the dominant community orientation. For example, I have known senior local government practitioners who thrive in settings in which the dominant orientation is toward small, limited government with submissive and compliant public professionals. I have also known practitioners who, in the same sort of environment, feel that their talents are wasted and their creativity suppressed.

Some settings can be sufficiently difficult that only a very resilient practitioner will succeed. As an example, I knew a city planning director in a medium-sized Western community whose conditions of work changed dramatically following a local city council election. The community could be characterized as one with a relatively closed governance structure, marketplace orientation, preference for a restricted government role, and a sometimes resistant attitude toward public professionalism. Nevertheless, for several years the governing body was dominated by a group that took a somewhat broader, more progressive stance toward governance than might be reflected in a true assessment of prevailing community opinion.

After the election, the council was dominated by a group that wanted to dramatically reduce the influence of the city's public professionals and shift the policy orientation away from a balance between the marketplace and living environment orientations to a strong marketplace orientation. This group would have liked to replace the planning director with someone more inclined toward their point of view, but they were unable to accomplish this. Instead, they did their best to let him know that he was expected to play a subordinate role in governance. At a council meeting, the mayor publicly ordered the planning director not to look at citizens who were speaking from a podium during hearings on land-use matters. The director was told to look straight ahead instead of turning to look at speakers, because he might intimidate them.

This was only one incident, symptomatic of the working environment of this practitioner in a situation in which the dominant community orientation toward governance had changed. A practitioner who had always worked in such an environment might not experience a negative reaction. For a person accustomed to an environment more favorable to professionalism this could be a serious shock, leading to such stress and dissatisfaction that the practitioner would withdraw from engagement with the community, simply marking time, or leave for another job.

In sum, each community has its unique set of public policy orientations that change over time and have significant effects on the public lives of citizens, representatives, and practitioners. An awareness of these orientations can help people involved in governance choose how they wish to approach their roles and the actions they take toward fulfilling their goals. Community orientations should not be thought of as absolute constraints preventing certain actions, but as a framework that defines possibilities and that can be changed by participants in the public policy process.

Citizens, Representatives, and Practitioners

Community Citizenship

In Chapter 3, we discussed several important ideas about citizenship, including the *individualistic, or classical liberal* view, and the *collectivistic, or classical republican,* view. These views were significant in the era of the founding of the nation and are prominent in contemporary politics at all levels of government. Americans are interested in preserving individual liberty and freedom from government control, but they also seek a sense of community, a sense of larger purpose and collective public action.

These views of citizenship are reflected in three basic citizenship roles, the *freerider, watchdog,* and *activist.* The freerider knows little about and does not take part in community affairs, allowing others to serve as his or her surrogates. The watchdog pays attention to community events and politics, but becomes personally involved only if something happens that directly affects her or his life. The activist is committed to an active public life and participates on boards and committees, attends meetings, and is an important part of community policy making and implementation.

The Citizen Governance model is intended to help in creating genuine citizen self-governance. Creating citizen self-governance in communities requires attention to the dynamics of citizen participation. The *critical theory* perspective makes us aware that there are different interests in the community and that the public often is relatively unaware of the public policy process and its implications for their lives. For public decision making on policy issues to be of good quality, citizens must be able to gain access to information and take part in deliberations that are open, welcoming, and informed, and where the contributions of each person are valued regardless of status or position. Because community elites may not want this sort of open deliberative process to occur, public service practitioners must decide whether to follow the directives that flow from representative government or to assume the risk of working directly with citizens to promote enlightened citizen governance.

Citizen governance is often seen by representatives and public professionals as threatening to their interests. Citizens who want to take part in policy making may be viewed by representatives as interfering with their lawful decision-making authority. Citizens and representatives who want to take part in decision making about program implementation may be viewed by practitioners as micro-managing. However, for the democracy and accountability principles to be fulfilled, citizens must be a part of policy making, and representatives and citizens must be a part of implementation. For citizens, representatives, or practitioners to make informed decisions about public services they need to remain within the boundaries of the individual knowledge limit. The IKL requires that citizens who govern and professionals who administer public services understand the types of daily tasks performed by practitioners who deliver the services. Application of the IKL leads to fulfillment of the scale principle, because accountable and rational policy and decision making takes place at a level of authority close to the actual work of service or program delivery.

Outside the government organization, this means creation of citizen involvement structures that allow neighborhood residents to take part in decision making affecting their area of interest. Inside organizations, it means formation of ongoing *citizen boards and committees* charged with policy making and implementation of public programs, subject to review, revision, and approval by the elected representatives who are the governing body.

Community Representation

Because of the size and complexity of government, all but the very smallest communities must use a *representative* form of government rather than a *direct democracy*. An elected representative can choose to act as a *delegate* of the people, striving to sense majority public opinion and vote accordingly, or as a *trustee* of the public interest, seeking to identify a longer-term vision of what would be best for the community.

Just as each member of a governing body decides how her or she wishes to represent the public, so too does each governing body have its own unique character. We can identify three basic types of governing body: the delegate, the advocate, and the trustee. The *delegate governing body* seeks to carry out the majority public will; *the advocate body* pursues particular policy goals; and *the trustee body* views its role as defining and implementing the broad public interest.

"Failure of representation" occurs when an elected governing body appears to make decisions that are not in the public interest.

This could happen because of control of the public policy process by certain individuals or groups or because the individual knowledge limit, and the accountability and rationality principles are violated when governing body members do not have sufficient knowledge of the services they are expected to govern. The potential for failure of representation is always present. Though the relationship between a governing body and citizens may be a healthy one at a given point in time, it can change as new issues emerge or an election changes the composition and interests of the body. The presence of this potential for failure of representation means that there is a "burden of representation," a way of expressing the reality that heavy reliance on a single small group of people to represent the best interests of an entire community can be of serious concern.

The creation of citizen boards to oversee service functions takes some of this burden from the governing body, broadening the base of citizens involved in policy making and implementation. However, the problem of delegation of authority remains. So long as the governing body is thought to be the place where most important decisions are made, the problem of failure of representation is still present. Put another way, concentrating decision making about community services in one body violates the individual knowledge limit and the accountability and rationality principles. If a group of representatives cannot fully understand those things they are called on to decide, their decisions will often be inaccurate and irrational, and no one will be directly accountable for the consequences. Also, such decision making often takes place in a public hearing setting with a crowded agenda so that the public has little opportunity to take part in a meaningful dialogue about a proposed policy. In this way, centralized decision making by the governing body violates the democracy principle as well.

This problem can be addressed by distinguishing between *routine* and *community interest policy*. The governing body is the appropriate place for two types of policy decisions to be made: routine decisions that should be made by representatives rather than public professionals but that do not require full citizen involvement, such as approving a service contract or choosing a medical insurance plan for employees; and review and final approval of the decisions of citizen boards. This review can be on appeal by parties involved in a controversy or simply part of the normal process of policy making in which major community decisions are discussed by the governing body prior to approval.

The governing body that serves as routine decision maker and reviewer of the actions of citizens gives up its perceived control of the public policy agenda. Instead of insisting on being the sole interpreter of the public interest, they become a *community coordinating council*, stewards of a community-wide process of discourse and decision making on matters affecting the public life of the community. They ensure that citizen concerns and matters of the efficient management of community affairs are directed to the appropriate citizen board and that the board and its practitioner staff are held accountable for positive results. They ensure that in each functional area, the citizen board and practitioners create an open and welcoming discourse setting in which the democracy principle can be fulfilled. In these ways, public policy creation and implementation become the "property" of the community as a whole.

Community Public Practice

We found, in Chapter 5, that contemporary professional public service has grown throughout the nation's history. It began with local residents who would volunteer to perform basic community tasks, such as repairing roads, keeping the peace, recording town business, or catching wayward livestock. As communities grew, residents would be paid a small amount to make such work more attractive and to compensate for the additional time involved because of community size. Later, many of these service functions grew into full-time jobs until, in the nineteenth century, a variety of occupational fields (such as police and fire, public health, education, and public works) began to develop the work content and organizational structure with which we are familiar today. At this point, a distinction became clear between citizens and the *public service practitioner*, whereby practitioners devote their work lives to public service rather than performing public service as a part-time activity.

With this development, the roles of public service practitioners became different from those of the people they served. When public service was performed by citizens volunteering their time, the adequacy of their performance was judged by other citizens in similar circumstances. In evaluating their neighbors' performance of public tasks, they judged one small but important part of a person's social life within the community. The emergence of full-time public service meant that the entire work life of the public service practitioner was evaluated by many people, peers, subordinates, superiors in the bureaucratic hierarchy, citizens, and elected representatives. In this situation, the practitioner's *sphere of discretion* is determined by the *role expectations* held by the *role set*. Each practitioner's role is subject to change over time as members of the role set change, events alter perceptions of the practitioner's role or the needs of the community, or the practitioner or members of the role set renegotiate the content of the role.

Public service practitioners pursue a variety of *substantive professional goals,* depending on their occupational specialties and personal preferences. These goals help to define the relationship between practitioners and their role sets. I have identified five broad areas of professional concern to community public service practitioners. The first is the traditional goal of *value-free neutrality,* based on the reform concept, from the late nineteenth and twentieth centuries, of separating the determination of policy from its implementation. The second is the goal of *legitimacy,* of building authority and status for public administration in society. The third is the goal of *sustainability,* finding a balance between economic development and the environment. The fourth is *social equity,* seeking to deal with the impacts of the economic system on those at the lower end of the economic scale. The fifth is to *facilitate citizen discourse,* to create an open and welcoming setting for self-governance.

The range of practitioner responses to the challenge of shaping a role within a particular community environment can be expressed in the typology of the *implementer, helper, and controller*. The implementer provides competent professional service while attempting to keep away from the policy-making process; this is the traditional neutrality model. The controller works to influence the policy process in favor of a specific substantive goal, sometimes stepping outside the expected boundaries of the practitioner role in an attempt to influence the actions of superiors, representatives, or citizens.

The helper provides professional service like the implementer and may care deeply about substantive policy goals. However, unlike the controller, the helper chooses to assist citizens to become fully self-governing. Helpers accomplish this by providing citizens with the information they need to make rational decisions and by working to create an open and welcoming discourse setting. In doing this the helper gives away the power of controlling the policy-making process, yet becomes even more valued and useful to the community. Thus, paradoxically, giving away the professional need to control the policy process brings the practitioner greater opportunities to serve the public interest and the democracy and rationality principles.

Making Citizen Governance Work

Overview

The reader might well think that implementing Citizen Governance could be a difficult challenge. The model asks for a rethinking of working relationships and potentially stressful changes in roles and structures. People naturally think and act incrementally—that is, they like to move forward one step at a time, checking for the effects of their actions and trying to alter course where such effects are especially troubling. More dramatic change can be frightening or threatening.

Citizen Governance is about constructive change that involves people in making their communities work, so the process of change should move one step at a time, giving people time to deliberate and offer suggestions about the pace and scope of the innovations. Having outside experts facilitate work toward Citizen Governance may be helpful, especially where there is disagreement about how to proceed. However, it should be kept in mind that community members are the people who matter in this process, and they need to both retain control and take responsibility for the outcome.

The Principles of Community Governance as Guide

The four principles of community governance should be used as a constant guide and test of proposals for change. At each decision point, people should ask the following questions.

- *Scale.* Are we acting at the lowest possible level consistent with accomplishing our goals?
- *Democracy.* Are we providing an open and welcoming opportunity for interested citizens to participate meaningfully in policy making and implementation?
- *Accountability.* Are we structuring administration of services and programs in a way that links performance to citizen wishes?
- *Rationality.* Are we ensuring that sufficient time, thought, and respect for all views are incorporated into decision making and implementation?

Commitment

Moving toward Citizen Governance is an important step in the life of the community. The governing body has the responsibility to decide whether to change from a centralized model of governance to a citizen-centered model. For the change process to be successful, elected representatives must be certain it is the right course and be committed to the changes that will come, changes in their role and the roles of citizens and professionals.

This commitment should be made following discussion as a group and individually with concerned citizens and public professionals. It is not a commitment to plunge ahead regardless of resistance or problems, but a commitment to begin a process of transforming community governance to meet the new realities of the twenty-first century.

Elements of Citizen Governance

The three basic elements of Citizen Governance are listed next. These are general ideas about changing the roles of the governing body, citizens, and practitioners to better fulfill the principles of Community Governance. Exactly how they are carried out will vary according to each community's situation.

- *The Coordinating Council.* Move elected governing bodies from a "central decision making" role to a "citizen's coordinating" role; redefine the governing body's duties from deciding most issues to delegating issues to citizen boards, hearing their recommendations, and affirming or modifying their work to fit overall community goals.
- *The Citizen's Boards.* Create citizen advisory boards to assist in administering major local government functions, such as police, fire, utilities, public works, parks and recreation, and social services. In larger jurisdictions, divide these broad functions into subareas and create citizen boards for each.
- *The Helper.* Change the role of public service practitioners from controlling public bureaucracies to assisting citizens in understanding community issues and services, helping them to make informed decisions about public programs, and carrying out daily tasks of implementation. This role recognizes the necessity for expertise in administration—not expertise that controls and excludes, but expertise that allows citizens to create and deliver the kind of services they want.

Creating the Structure

Here are some steps to follow in thinking about the structures to be used with Citizen Governance. It might be wise to form a standing Committee on Citizen Governance, or CCG, to assist in creating the structures and to evaluate progress at periodic intervals, suggesting changes in implementation when needed. The membership could include citizens, staff members, one or more governing body representatives and, when new citizen boards are formed, the chairs of those boards. Of course, the steps taken will be different in each community, but the intent is to go through the process listed. Implementation might be phased so that one or a few program areas could be used as a pilot project to determine how well Citizen Governance works.

1. List the services and programs the community government offers, then examine each one to see which would benefit from a citizen board. Not all services and programs need citizen oversight and participation in implementation, as some do not usually involve policy matters that could be thought of as being of community interest.

2. Determine the appropriate number or size of service that ought to be assigned to each board, using the individual knowledge limit. Roughly, imagine the size and number of program functions a new board member could come to understand in some detail after a year of service; that is probably about the right number of functions for that particular board to handle, while fulfilling the accountability and rationality principles.

3. Think about the composition of each citizen board in relation to size, terms of office, balancing of views, and geographic representation. It is wise to specify representation by profession if specialized competence is needed, for example on a board that oversees water or sewer systems. At the same time, citizen boards should remain just that—citizen boards, not professional review bodies—and people with related professional training should not dominate boards. Neither should people with specific, self-interested agendas.

4. Work out the formal charge to each board, including the role of the governing body and the sphere of responsibility of each board and the practitioners who will provide staff assistance. Staff should always be regarded as valued members of the group, people with special expertise, a sense of the history of the organization and the program(s), and knowledge of the ways such programs have been operated successfully in other times and places. This is a matter of balance. The size of a board should be large enough to gain participation and representation, small

enough for effective decision making. Term length should allow enough time for board members to become informed, yet be short enough to prevent burnout and allow new people to take part.

5. The process of creating and implementing a citizen governance structure works best alongside a citizen involvement program outside the organization, such as neighborhood organizations and committees dealing with particular issues. It is best to have both "inside" and "outside" processes operating because they share in common the values of the principles of Community Governance and are complementary.

Implementation

Implementation is a crucial stage. It is a good time to reinforce the idea that the governing body and the CCG must act in a deliberate manner that is considerate of the views of the people involved. At the same time, everyone needs to understand that it is quite possible that significant changes and corrections will be needed along the way. People cannot foresee all possibilities, needs, and problems, so they need to accept their fallibility and be open to modifying the system based on the principles of Community Governance. Here are five steps toward implementing Citizen Governance.

1. *Formalize the Structure.* Put into resolution or ordinance form the directives needed to allocate authority and responsibility to boards (or neighborhood or other outside organizations) and to require agency personnel to serve them appropriately. Build in plenty of flexibility and room to adapt to experience and circumstances. If appropriate, move in slow and incremental steps, trying out the new ideas as pilot projects.

2. *Train the Staff.* Work with staff to re-orient them from the bureaucratic control model to the helper model of citizen interaction and service. Insist on abandonment of defensive "us-versus-them" views of citizens or "bean-counting" bureaucratic inflexibility, replacing them with commitment to service, of professional work as an act of enhancing citizen satisfaction as the owners of their community. This is not just a matter of pleasing customers,

but of creating a setting in which community residents can truly self-govern.

3. *Train the Board Members.* Work with citizens to acquaint them with their roles and spheres of responsibility. Make clear that professional staff are trusted advisers and experts, not the controllers of agencies or the keepers of the secrets of expert knowledge. Also, staff should not be used as scapegoats to be blamed or harassed for things beyond their control.

4. *Resolve Issues.* As the new Citizen Governance process begins, assist in resolving questions about duties and responsibilities, smoothing the process and allowing staff and citizens to settle effectively into their new roles. Create a regular schedule of meetings between the CCG and the governing body. Use any other reporting or joint membership arrangements that will help foster open and frequent communication.

5. *Make Mid-Course Corrections.* The governing body should be ready to revise the structure and the processes as experience suggests the need for change. The new structure may in some areas prove to be too decentralized, causing problems of coordination and accountability, or it may be necessary to further decentralize because one or more boards have too many functions to oversee. Special interests may come to dominate a board and action may be needed to restore a balance of views. Training may need adjustment based on performance of participants, the relationships between citizens and the governing body may need fine tuning, and so on. In all cases, changes should stay close to the principles and elements of the Citizen Governance model.

Conclusion

This brings us to the end of our presentation of Citizen Governance. I hope you have found the conceptual material interesting, the overall concept exciting, and the specific suggestions for implementation useful and practical. Returning to complete the circle begun in Chapter 1, I believe these ideas can serve to bring the practice of community governance closer to the people and to the coming reality of the twenty-first century.

References

Abney, Glenn, and Thomas P. Lauth. 1986. *The politics of state and city administration*. Albany: State University of New York Press.

Adams, Guy B., Priscilla V. Bowerman, Kenneth M. Dolbeare, and Camilla Stivers. 1990. Joining purpose to practice: A democratic identity for the public service. In *Images and identities in public administration*, ed. Henry D. Kass and Bayard L. Catron, 219–40. Newbury Park, Calif.: Sage.

Adrian, Charles R. 1958. A study of three communities. *Public Administration Review* 18 (Summer): 208–13.

———. 1988. Forms of city government in American history. Chapter in *The Municipal Year Book*. Washington, D.C.: International City Management Association.

Adrian, Charles R., and Ernest S. Griffith. 1976. *A history of American city government. Vol. 2, The formation of traditions, 1775–1870*. New York: Praeger.

Anglin, Roland. 1990. Diminishing utility: The effect on citizen preferences for local growth. *Urban Affairs Quarterly* 25 (June): 684–96.

Bachrach, Peter, and Morton S. Baratz. 1962. The two faces of power. *American Political Science Review* 56 (December): 947–52.

Bailey, Stephen K. 1964. Ethics and the public service. *Public Administration Review* 23 (December): 234–43.

Barber, Benjamin. 1984. *Strong democracy: Participatory politics for a new age*. Berkeley: University of California Press.

Bellah, Robert N., Richard Madsen, William M. Sullivan, Ann Swidler, and Steven M. Tipton. 1985. *Habits of the heart: Individualism and commitment in American life*. New York: Harper and Row.

Berkowitz, Peter. 1995. Communitarian criticisms and liberal lessons. *The ResponsiveCommunity* 5 (Fall): 54–64.

Berry, Jeffrey M., Kent E. Portney, and Ken Thomson. 1993. *The rebirth of urban democracy.* Washington, D.C.: Brookings Institution.

Blodgett, Terrell. 1994. Beware the lure of the "strong" mayor. *Public Management* 76 (January): 6–11.

Box, Richard C. 1990. The economic model of administrative behavior in local government. DPA dissertation, University of Southern California.

_____. 1993. Resistance to professional managers in American local government. *American Review of Public Administration* 23 (December): 403–18.

_____. 1995a. Critical theory and the paradox of discourse. *American Review of Public Administration* 25 (March): 1–19.

_____. 1995b. Optimistic view of the future of community governance. *Administrative Theory and Praxis* 17(1): 87–91.

_____. 1995c. Searching for the best structure for American local government. *International Journal of Public Administration* 18(4): 711–41.

Boynton, Robert Paul, and Deil S. Wright. 1971. Mayor-manager relationships in large council-manager cities: A reinterpretation. *Public Administration Review* 31 (January/February): 28–36.

Burns, Nancy. 1994. *The formation of American local governments: Private values in public institutions.* Oxford: Oxford University Press.

Conte, Christopher R. 1995. Teledemocracy for better or worse. *Governing* 8 (June): 33–41.

Cook, Edward M. 1976. *The fathers of the towns: Leadership and community structure in eighteenth-century New England.* Baltimore: Johns Hopkins University Press.

Cooper, Terry L. 1984. Public administration in an age of scarcity: A citizenship role for public administrators. In *Politics and administration: Woodrow Wilson and American public administration,* ed. Jack Rabin and James S. Bowman, 297–314. New York: Marcel Dekker.

_____. 1991. *An ethic of citizenship for public administration.* Englewood Cliffs, N.J.: Prentice Hall.

Craig, Stephen C. 1993. *The malevolent leaders: Popular discontent in America.* Boulder, Colo.: Westview Press.

Dahl, Robert A. 1961. *Who governs? Democracy and power in an American city.* New Haven, Conn.: Yale University Press.

Dewey, John. 1927/1985. *The public and its problems.* Athens, Ohio: Swallow Press.

Downs, Anthony. 1957. *An economic theory of democracy.* New York: Harper and Row.

Eberly, Don E. ed. 1994. *Building a community of citizens: Civil society in the 21st century.* Lanham, Md.: University Press of America.

Eisenhardt, Kathleen M. 1989. Agency theory: An assessment and review. *Academy of Management Review* 14(1): 57–74.

Elder, Shirley. 1992. Running a town the 17th-century way. *Governing* 5 (March): 29–30.

Etzioni, Amitai. 1992. Communitarian solutions/what communitarians think. *The Journal of State Government* 65 (January–March): 9–11.

_____, ed. 1995. *Rights and the common good: The communitarian perspective*. New York: St. Martin's Press.

Fannin, William R. 1983. City manager policy roles as a source of city council/city manager conflict. *International Journal of Public Administration* 5(4): 381–99.

Fisher, Robert. 1981. From grass-roots organizing to community service: Community organization practice in the community center movement, 1907–1930. In *Community organization for urban social change: A historical perspective*, ed. Robert Fisher and Peter Romanofsky, 33–58. Westport, Conn.: Greenwood Press.

Flentje, H. Edward, and Wendla Counihan. 1984. Running a "reformed" city: The hiring and firing of city managers. *Urban Resources* 2 (Fall): 9–14.

Follett, Mary Parker. 1918. *The new state: Group organization the solution of popular government*. New York: Longmans, Green.

Fox, Charles J., and Clarke E. Cochran. 1990. Discretion advocacy in public administration: Toward a Platonic guardian class? *Administration & Society* 22 (August): 249–71.

Fox, Charles J., and Hugh T. Miller. 1995. *Postmodern public administration: Toward discourse*. Thousand Oaks, Calif.: Sage.

Frisby, Michele, and Monica Bowman. 1996. What we have is a failure to communicate: The case for citizen involvement in local government decision making. *Public Management* 78 (February): A1–A5.

Gale, Dennis E. 1992. Eight state-sponsored growth management programs: A comparative analysis. *Journal of the American Planning Association* 58 (Autumn): 425–39.

Geuss, Raymond. 1981. *The idea of a critical theory: Habermas and the Frankfurt School*. Cambridge: Cambridge University Press.

Giddens, Anthony. 1984. *The constitution of society: Outline of the theory of structuration*. Berkeley: University of California Press.

Goodnow, Frank J. 1904/1991. *City government in the United States*. Holmes Beach, Fla.: Wm. W. Gaunt & Sons.

Goodsell, Charles. 1996. A memo to the public employees of America. *Administrative Theory and Praxis* 18(1): 48–49.

Gould, John. 1940. *New England town meeting: Safeguard of democracy*. Brattleboro, Vt.: Stephen Daye Press.

Griffith, Ernest S. 1938. *History of American city government. Vol. 1, The colonial period*. New York: Oxford University Press.

_____. 1974. *A history of American city government*. Vol. 3, The conspicuous failure, 1870–1900. New York: Praeger.

Gulick, Luther. 1937. Notes on the theory of organization. In *Classics of public administration*, 3d ed., ed. Jay M. Shafritz and Albert C. Hyde, 1992. Pacific Grove, CA: Brooks/Cole.

Gurwitt, Rob. 1992. A government that runs on citizen power. *Governing* 6 (December): 48–54.

_____. 1993a. The lure of the strong mayor. *Governing* 6 (July): 36–41.

_____. 1993b. Communitarianism: You can try it at home. *Governing* 6 (August): 33–9.

Habermas, Jurgen. 1970. *Toward a rational society: Student protest, science, and politics*. Boston: Beacon Press.

Harrigan, John J. 1989. *Political change in the metropolis.* 4th ed. Glenview, Ill.: Scott, Foresman.

Hill, B. W., ed. 1976. *Edmund Burke: On government, politics, and society.* New York: International Publications Service.

Hummel, Ralph P. 1987. *The bureaucratic experience.* 3d ed. New York: St. Martin's Press.

Hunter, Floyd. 1953. *Community power structure.* Chapel Hill: University of North Carolina Press.

Jefferson, Thomas. 1984. January 8, 1789 letter to Richard Price. In *Thomas Jefferson, writings,* ed. Merrill D. Peterson, 1935. New York: Literary Classics of the United States.

Johnson, David B. 1991. *Public choice: An introduction to the new political economy.* Mountain View, Calif.: Mountain View.

Joyce, Michael S. 1994. Citizenship in the 21st century: Individual self-government. In *Building a community of citizens: Civil society in the 21st century,* ed. Don E. Eberly, 3–10. Lanham, Md.: University Press of America.

Kass, Henry D., and Bayard L. Catron, eds. 1990. *Images and identities in public administration.* Newbury Park, Calif.: Sage.

Kaufman, Herbert. 1969. Administrative decentralization and political power. *Public Administration Review* 29 (January/February): 3–15.

Kemmis, Daniel. 1990. *Community and the politics of place.* Norman: University of Oklahoma Press.

King, Leslie, and Glenn Harris. 1989. Local responses to rapid rural growth. *Journal of the American Planning Association* 55 (Spring): 181–91.

Lappe, Frances Moore, and Paul Martin Du Bois. 1994. *The quickening of America: Rebuilding our nation, remaking our lives.* San Francisco: Jossey-Bass.

Lasch, Christopher. 1996. *The revolt of the elites and the betrayal of democracy.* New York: W.W. Norton.

Lockridge, Kenneth A. 1970/1985. *A New England town the first hundred years: Dedham, Massachusetts, 1636–1736.* New York: W.W. Norton.

Logan, John R., and Harvey L. Molotch. 1987. *Urban fortunes: The political economy of place.* Berkeley: University of California Press.

Lord, George F., and Albert C. Price. 1992. Growth ideology in a period of decline: Deindustrialization and restructuring, Flint style. *Social Problems* 39 (May): 155–69.

Loveridge, Ronald O. 1971. *City managers in legislative politics.* New York: Bobbs-Merrill.

Lowery, David, Ruth Hoogland DeHoog, and William E. Lyons. 1992. Citizenship in the empowered locality: An elaboration, a critique, and a partial test. *Urban Affairs Quarterly* 28 (September): 69–103.

Mansbridge, Jane. 1980. *Beyond adversary democracy.* New York: Basic Books.

Martin, Lawrence L. 1993. American county government: An historical perspective. In *County governments in an era of change,* ed. David R. Berman, 1–13. Westport, Conn.: Greenwood Press.

Massialas, Byron G. 1990. Educating students for conflict resolution and democratic decision making. *The Social Studies* 81 (September/October): 202–5.

Matthews, Richard K. 1986. *The radical politics of Thomas Jefferson: A revisionist view.* Lawrence: University Press of Kansas.

McDonald, Forrest. 1985. *Novus ordo seclorum: The intellectual origins of the Constitution.* Lawrence: University Press of Kansas.

McDonald, Lee Cameron. 1968. *Western political theory.* New York: Harcourt Brace Jovanovich.

Moe, Terry M. 1984. The new economics of organization. *American Journal of Political Science* 28 (November): 739–77.

Molotch, Harvey L. 1976. The city as a growth machine: Toward a political economy of place. *American Journal of Sociology* 82 (September): 309–32.

Morison, Samuel Eliot. 1965. *The Oxford history of the American people.* New York: Oxford University Press.

Nalbandian, John. 1989. The contemporary role of city managers. *American Review of Public Administration* 19 (December): 261–78.

Nelson, Arthur C. 1992. Preserving prime farmland in the face of urbanization. *Journal of the American Planning Association* 58 (Autumn): 467–88.

Nelson, Lisa S., and Louis F. Weschler. 1996. Community sustainability as a dimension of administrative ethics. *Administrative Theory and Praxis* 18(1): 13–26.

Nice, David C. 1987. *Federalism: The politics of intergovernmental relations.* New York: St. Martin's Press.

Niskanen, William A. 1971. *Bureaucracy and representative government.* Chicago: Aldine Atherton.

———. 1991. A reflection on bureaucracy and representative government. In *The budget-maximizing bureaucrat: Appraisals and evidence,* ed. Andre Blais and Stephane Dion, 13–31. Pittsburgh, Penn.: University of Pittsburgh Press.

Osborne, David, and Ted Gaebler. 1993. *Reinventing government: How the entrepreneurial spirit is transforming the public sector.* New York: Penguin Books.

Ostrom, Elinor. 1993. A communitarian approach to local governance. *National Civic Review* (Summer): 226–33.

Ostrom, Vincent, Charles M. Tiebout, and Robert Warren. 1961. The organization of government in metropolitan areas: A theoretical inquiry. *American Political Science Review* 55 (December): 831–42.

Pealy, Dorothee Strauss. 1958. The need for elected leadership. *Public Administration Review* 18 (Summer): 214–16.

Peterson, Paul E. 1981. *City limits.* Chicago: University of Chicago Press.

Phillips, Derek L. 1993. *Looking backward: A critical appraisal of communitarian thought.* Princeton, N.J.: Princeton University Press.

Protasel, Greg J. 1988. Abandonments of the council-manager plan: A new institutionalist perspective. *Public Administration Review* 48 (July/August): 807–12.

Rodgers, Daniel T. 1979. *The work ethic in industrial America, 1850–1920.* Chicago: University of Chicago Press.

Rodgers, Joseph Lee. 1977. *Citizen committees: A guide to their use in local government.* Cambridge, Mass.: Ballinger.

Rohr, John A. 1986. *Ethics for bureaucrats: An essay on law and values.* New York: Marcel Dekker.

———. 1993. Toward a more perfect union. *Public Administration Review* 53 (May/June): 246–9.

Ross, Bernard H., and Myron A. Levine. 1996. *Urban politics: Power in metropolitan America.* 5th ed. Itasca, Ill.: F.E. Peacock.

Ross, Bernard H., Myron A. Levine, and Murray S. Stedman. 1991. *Urban politics: Power in metropolitan America.* 4th ed. Itasca, Illinois: F. E. Peacock Publishers.

Rossiter, Clinton, ed. 1961. *The federalist papers.* New York: New American Library.

Rousseau, Jean-Jacques. 1762/1978. *On the social contract.* Ed. by Roger D. Masters, trans. by Judith R. Masters. New York: St. Martin's Press.

Saltzstein, Alan L. 1974. City managers and city councils: Perceptions of the division of authority. *The Western Political Quarterly* 27 (March): 275–88.

Schachter, Hindy Lauer. 1997. *Reinventing government or reinventing ourselves.* Albany: State University of New York Press.

Schattschneider, E. E. 1975. *The semisovereign people: A realist's view of democracy in America.* Hinsdale, Ill.: Dryden Press.

Schlesinger, Arthur M. 1986. *The cycles of American history.* Boston: Houghton Mifflin.

Schneider, Mark, and Paul Teske. 1993a. The antigrowth entrepreneur: Challenging the "equilibrium" of the growth machine. *The Journal of Politics* 55 (August): 720–36.

_____. 1993b. The progrowth entrepreneur in local government. *Urban Affairs Quarterly* 29 (December): 316–27.

Schon, Donald A. 1983. *The reflective practitioner: How professionals think in action.* New York: Basic Books.

Scott, William G., and David K. Hart. 1979. *Organizational America.* Boston: Houghton Mifflin.

Selznick, Philip. 1992. *The moral commonwealth: Social theory and the promise of community.* Berkeley: University of California Press.

Shefter, Martin. 1985. *Political crisis/fiscal crisis: The collapse and revival of New York City.* New York: Basic Books.

Sheldon, Garrett Ward. 1993. *The political philosophy of Thomas Jefferson.* Baltimore: Johns Hopkins University Press.

Sinopoli, Richard C. 1992. *The foundations of American citizenship: Liberalism, the Constitution, and civic virtue.* Oxford: Oxford University Press.

Smith, Page. 1966. *As a city upon a hill: The town in American history.* New York: Alfred A. Knopf.

Sparrow, Glen. 1985. The emerging chief executive: The San Diego experience. *National Civic Review* 74 (December): 538–47.

Spicer, Michael W., and Larry D. Terry. 1993. Legitimacy, history, and logic: Public administration and the Constitution. *Public Administration Review* 53 (May/June): 239–46.

Stene, Edwin O., and George K. Floro. 1953. *Abandonments of the manager plan: A study of four small cities.* Lawrence: University of Kansas Governmental Research Center.

Stone, Clarence N. 1993. Urban regimes and the capacity to govern: A political economy approach. *Journal of Urban Affairs* 15(1): 1–28.

Stillman, Richard J. 1974. *The rise of the city manager: A public professional in local government.* Albuquerque: University of New Mexico Press.

_____. 1995. *The American bureaucracy: The core of modern government.* 2d ed. Chicago: Nelson-Hall Publishers.

Stivers, Camilla. 1990. The public agency as polis: Active citizenship in the administrative state. *Administration & Society* 22 (May): 86–105.

_____. 1993. Rationality and romanticism in Constitutional argument. *Public Administration Review* 53 (May/June): 254–7.

Storing, Herbert J. 1981. *What the Anti-Federalists were for.* Chicago: University of Chicago Press.

Svara, James H. 1986a. Contributions of the city council to effective governance. *Popular Government* 51 (Spring): 1–8.

_____. 1986b. The mayor in council-manager cities: Recognizing leadership potential. *National Civic Review* 75 (September-October): 271–305.

_____. 1990. *Official leadership in the city: Patterns of conflict and cooperation.* Oxford: Oxford University Press.

Terry, Larry D. 1993. Why we should abandon the misconceived quest to reconcile public entrepreneurship with democracy: A response to Bellone and Goerl's "Reconciling public entrepreneurship and democracy." *Public Administration Review* 53 (July/August): 393–5.

Thomas, John Clayton. 1986. *Between citizen and city: Neighborhood organizations and urban politics in Cincinnati.* Lawrence: University Press of Kansas.

Thompson, Victor A. 1975. *Without sympathy or enthusiasm: The problem of administrative compassion.* University: University of Alabama Press.

Tiebout, Charles M. 1956. A pure theory of local expenditures. *The Journal of Political Economy* 64 (October): 416–24.

de Tocqueville, Alexis. 1969. *Democracy in America.* Ed. by J.P. Mayer, trans. by George Lawrence. Garden City, N.Y.: Doubleday.

Verba, Sidney, and Norman H. Nie. 1972. *Participation in America: Political democracy and social equality.* New York: Harper and Row.

Vogel, Ronald K., and Bert E. Swanson. 1989. The growth machine versus the antigrowth coalition: The battle for our communities. *Urban Affairs Quarterly* 25 (September): 63–85.

Waldo, Dwight. 1981. *The enterprise of public administration: A summary view.* Novato, Calif.: Chandler and Sharp.

Wamsley, Gary L., Charles T. Goodsell, John A. Rohr, Camilla M. Stivers, Orion F. White, and James F. Wolf. 1987. The public administration and the governance process: Refocusing the American dialogue. In *A centennial history of the American administrative state,* ed. Ralph C. Chandler, 291–317. New York: Free Press.

Warren, Kenneth F. 1993. We have debated ad nauseum the legitimacy of the administrative state—but why? *Public Administration Review* 53 (May/June): 249–54.

Waste, Robert J., ed. 1986. *Community power: Directions for future research.* Beverly Hills: Sage.

_____. 1989. *The ecology of policy making.* Oxford: Oxford University Press.

_____. 1993. City limits, pluralism, and urban political economy. *Journal of Urban Affairs* 15(5): 445–55.

White, Louise G. 1982. Improving the goal-setting process in local government. *Public Administration Review* 42 (January/February): 77–83.

Whitt, J. Allen, and John C. Lammers. 1991. The art of growth: Ties between development organizations and the performing arts. *Urban Affairs Quarterly* 26 (March): 376–93.

Wikstrom, Nelson. 1979. The mayor as policy leader in the council-manager form of government: A view from the field. *Public Administration Review* 39 (May/June): 270–6.

Williams, Oliver P., and Charles R. Adrian. 1963. *Four cities: A study in comparative policy making.* Philadelphia: University of Pennsylvania Press.

Wilson, Woodrow. 1887. The study of administration. In *Classics of public administration,* ed. Jay M. Shafritz and Albert C. Hyde, 11–24. 3d ed. Pacific Grove, Calif.: Brooks/Cole.

Yankelovich, Daniel. 1991. *Coming to public judgment: Making democracy work in a complex world.* Syracuse, N.Y.: Syracuse University Press.

Zuckerman, Michael. 1970. *Peaceable kingdoms: New England towns in the eighteenth century.* New York: Alfred A. Knopf.

Index

About the Author

Richard C. Box is Associate Professor of Public Administration in the Graduate School of Public Affairs, University of Colorado at Colorado Springs. He served for 13 years in local governments in Oregon and California as a planner, as a department head in the areas of planning, building safety, housing, and public works, and as a city manager. He completed his doctorate in Public Administration at the University of Southern California in 1990, the year in which he came to the University of Colorado at Colorado Springs.

Richard Box teaches several courses in the GSPA, including Introduction to Public Service, Financial Management, Human Resources Management, Local Government Politics, and Intergovernmental Management. His research focuses on the relationship between political responsiveness and professional rationality in a democratic society, and his work has been published in several national journals in the field of public administration. He has taken part in a variety of community activities, including serving on citizen committees examining community issues and making presentations on the theory and practice of areas of financial and personnel management, organizational structures, and the roles of professionals and elected officials. His community activities are directed toward improving the quality of public governance through open dialogue and citizen access to the public policy process.